Water Gardens

Other Books by Jacqueline Hériteau

The National Arboretum Book of Outstanding Garden Plants

The American Horticultural Society Flower Finder

A Feast of Soups

Potpourri and Other Fragrant Delights

A Feast of Flowers

Other Books by Charles B. Thomas

Water Gardens for Plants and Fish

Water Gardens

Jacqueline Hériteau

Charles B. Thomas

Houghton Mifflin Company   Boston / New York   1994

Copyright © 1994 by Jacqueline Hériteau and Charles B. Thomas

Library of Congress Cataloging-in-Publication Data
Hériteau, Jacqueline.
  Water gardens / Jacqueline Hériteau and Charles B. Thomas.
    p.   cm.
  Includes index.
  ISBN 0-395-65633-8
  1. Water gardens.   I. Thomas, Charles B. (Charles Brosius),
1936–   II. Title.
SB423.H455 1993   93-29675
635.9′674—dc20   CIP

Printed in Italy

Book design by Dianne Schaefer

NIL 10 9 8 7 6 5 4 3 2 1

. . . he leadeth me beside the still waters

Psalm 23:2

Acknowledgments

We are very grateful to our editor, Frances Tenenbaum, for help with the organization of the material and much else; to our publisher, Houghton Mifflin Company; to our manuscript editor, Peg Anderson; to literary agent Gail Ross; to Tom Robertson, word-processing guru; and to Karen O'Dell, who kept the manuscript moving between authors and did much of the photo research.

Our thanks to Kibbe and Simone Turner and to Craig Tufts for contributions to the section on attracting wildlife to a backyard water garden.

We wish to express our great appreciation for the invaluable suggestions offered by Ray Klinger; Walter Pagels, international aquatic plant collector; Perry Slocum of North Carolina, internationally acclaimed water lily and lotus breeder; Peter Slocum; Joseph Tomocik of Colorado, keeper of the most varied public water lily collection in North America; and Lilypons Water Gardens associates Rolf J. Nelson of Texas, and George L. Thomas III, Lisa Allen, Angela Elspas, and Shannon Stanton of Maryland.

Photograph Credits

Contents

Part One   The Pond

1   *Living with a Water Garden*   3
Four Steps to a New World
The Keepers of the Water Garden

2   *Siting the Garden*   15
Practical Considerations
Selecting a Water Garden
Pond Designs
A Few Do's and a Don't
Backyard Wildlife
Installing the Pond

3   *Clear, Beautiful Water*   37
Algae
pH and All That
Dechlorinating
Taking Pond Measurements

4   *Pumps, Filters, and the Sounds of Water*   51
Filters
Pumps
The Sounds of Water
Water at Night
Insurance Against Ice

5   *Planting, Stocking, and Maintaining the Garden*   65
The Magic Formula
Planting the Pond
The Submerged Plants
The Ornamental Plants
Releasing Fish and Other Small Helpers
Maintenance: The Pond Year

Part Two The Aquatic Plants and Pond Creatures

6 *Nymphaea: The Water Lilies*   85
   Shading the Pond
   Cutting Flowers
   The Best Hardy Lilies
   Planting, Culture, and Winter Care
   The Best Tropical Lilies
   Planting, Culture, and Winter Care

7 *The Small Floating-leaved Plants*   143
   The Best Small Floating-leaved Plants
   Planting, Culture, and Winter Care

8 *The Sacred Lotus and Other Nelumbos*   157
   Cutting Lotus Flowers
   The Best Lotus Varieties
   Planting, Culture, and Winter Care

9 *Framing the Water Garden*   173
   The Best Pond Irises
   The Best Narrow-leaved Verticals
   The Best Broad-leaved Verticals

10 *Fish, Snails, and Other Small Helpers*   209
   The Fish
   Snails
   Tadpoles and Frogs
   Turtles—Only for Love

Hardiness Zone Map   221
Appendix: Pronunciation of Botanical Names   222
Index   225

Part One
The Pond

1 🐚 Living with a Water Garden

Aquatic plants have seasons as compelling as those of a flower border. What draws you to the water garden day after day is the unfolding life of this small, self-sustaining world. (Photo by Ruth Askins)

A GARDEN POND is a small romantic Eden with floating flowers, fragrance, reflections, the sound of water, and the glint of golden fish. It is an oasis of serenity and an enchanting world of its own, complete with birds, butterflies, and dragonflies. Each element plays a vital role, and together they create an ecosystem, a living organism whose interacting parts express an exquisite, fascinating intelligence.

New pond owners usually are surprised to discover how important a daily visit to the water garden becomes. What draws you irresistibly is the unfolding life of this little universe. The pond's changing seasons are as compelling as those of any beautiful flower garden, but far more lively. In early spring, just after the forsythia and the first daffodils bloom, there comes a morning when you feel a new softness in the air. The snails stir a bit, waking to graze on the dark green algae that fuzzes the sides of the pond as the water warms. At noon the thermometer rises to 60 degrees, and by sunset you catch a glimpse of green where the water lilies are sleeping. Next day, from sunrise till noon, down among the submerged plants, the fish will be darting and ducking, courting and mating. That same day, the sun will outline grayish amber bubbles the size of a pinhead attached to the undulating fronds. Each is an individual mite of life.

As midspring approaches, the irises growing along the margins rise up and fly their blue and yellow flags. By late spring you are counting, like a miser his gold, the fat oval buds of the hardy water lilies, dreaming of moonlit summer evenings perfumed by the night-blooming tropical lilies. After six to eight weeks of warmth, lilies, lotus, spider lilies, water snowflake, canna, and the beautiful white pickerel rush open their multicolored show between blue sky and the water reflecting it. As summer advances, the fish grow, imperceptibly as children do, and though you visit them daily, it's late in the season or even early fall before you suddenly realize how much they have grown.

If you live in an area with a semitropical climate, such as Florida, the pond's life won't slow down until the coldest time of the year. But where autumn brings a real chill, the lily pads become streaked with yellow as gold and crimson take over the land plants. After the frost comes, the fish and the snails retreat to the bottom of the pond and the lily rhizomes subside into their winter nap. Freed of foliage cover, the open water reflects clouds and sky. Ice crystals lace its borders, and when snow drifts across its surface, it forms beautiful patterns. Even then, teeth chattering, blowing puffs of cloud, you'll want to go to the pond at certain times of day. There, cares vanish as you spend hours cataloging the changes. In every season, a water garden gives you a sense of wonder and peace and a certain strength.

A new water garden dappled by a summer shower: in a season or two the stony contours will green over, and then the pond and its watercourse will look as though nature had put them there. (Photo by George Grahe)

Four Steps to a New World

The factors that make a water garden successful have been carefully observed and are simple enough for any beginner to reproduce. If you set up the pond according to the rules nature created, the ecosystem will take over. A new water garden needs to be left alone for about six weeks in order to come into balance. Be patient. Do *less* rather than more during this period and the pond will arrange its elements in natural relationships to each other, creating the near-perfect balance that makes a delightful whole. Once the water garden is established, you should not have to spend more than an hour a month on routine plant maintenance — feeding them and removing yellowing foliage and spent blossoms.

This book addresses the typical home garden pond, or lily pond, contained by an artificial liner — usually rubber, plastic, fiberglass, or concrete. We do not include information on planting earth-bottomed ponds, which allow naturally spreading plants to become invasive and difficult to control. Such ponds are governed by various local, state, and federal wetland regulations. The agencies administering these regulations, and the county extension agents of land grant state universities, are qualified to advise you on what you may and may not do with wetlands.

Water gardens are generally between 15 and 30 inches deep and have a surface area of 20 to 200 square feet. The dimensions might be anywhere from 4 by 5 feet to 10 by 20 feet. A water garden can be planted in any watertight, nontoxic container, from something the size of a half barrel to a pond as large as you can fit on your property. The 200 outstanding plants recommended in Chapters 6 through 11 are the aquatic ornamentals that flourish in this type of water garden in a range of North American climates, including southern Florida, Texas, California, the cool Pacific Northwest, and Canada — climates with characteristics of USDA Zones 3 and 4 through frost-free Zone 11.

A new water garden comes together in four steps, which are described in detail in the next chapters.

1. You site, shape, dig, waterproof, and fill the pond. Most gardeners add a recirculating pump and a filter to freshen the water. By returning the water to the pond via a waterfall, piece of statuary, spray, or bubbler, the pump

adds two lovely elements to the water garden — the sight and sounds of moving water.

2. You set out the plants in soil containers at the correct depth for each plant. The only exceptions are a few small floating plants that live on the surface of the water.

3. You wait a week or two for the water to age. During that time the plants adjust, beneficial bacteria volunteer themselves, and algae begin to grow as the pond readies an environment for the small creatures that will complete a balanced ecosystem.

4. You release fish, snails, and, if you wish, other small helpers, such as frogs and tadpoles, into their new world to make their important contributions.

The Keepers of the Water Garden

The soul of a water garden is its living components, the plants and animals. Each element is necessary to the well-being of the whole, even certain bacteria. The beauty and health of the whole depends on the presence and well-being of each part. Their interactions maintain the balance of pond life, clear the water, keep the plants and flowers beautiful, and allow the fish to stay healthy.

Submerged Plants

Submerged plants, sometimes called oxygenating plants or grasses, are small and leafy and grow underwater. In a water garden they are planted in pans or pails which, as soon as the pond is filled with water, are distributed over the pond bottom. Strong allies in keeping the water beautiful and healthy for its inhabitants, they contribute oxygen and compete with algae for dissolved nutrients. One of their most important functions is to starve out the excess algae that makes water murky.

White snowflake, an aquatic plant with small, floating leaves, is one of the living elements that keep the water garden's ecosystem in balance.

Submerged plants also trap debris and are welcome spawning sites for fish. And they look graceful waving languidly from their underwater perches.

Water Lilies

There are two types of water lilies: the enchanting ones that are hardy in cold climates and the gorgeous tropicals. Their blossoms float on or above the water like many-petaled stars, surrounded by large, round pads, or leaves. Lilies are the center of attention in the aquatic garden and are the best source of color. In frost-free regions they bloom all year. In cooler areas they bloom all summer. Many varieties have a haunting perfume. But these beautiful plants also have a practical value in the pond's ecosystem. The floating foliage and flowers reduce the amount of sunlight reaching the water, thereby helping to keep the algae growth in check. Lilies also use up nutrients that otherwise would nourish undesirable algae and so contribute in a modest way to keeping the water clear and beautiful. The plants provide a place for fish to hide, and their shade helps to keep the water temperature down on hot days. Water lilies release oxygen to the atmosphere from the top of the leaf, unlike land plants, which breathe on the underside because their top surfaces get dusty.

Small Plants with Floating Leaves

A number of plants that float dainty leaves and flowers are used in pond design. The delicate green patterns creep out over the reflective surface of the water and bring welcome shade to underwater areas between the lily pads and the lotus. They remove minor amounts of the nutrients that otherwise would be claimed by unwanted algae. But their major gift is a delightful contrast in texture and form to the big floating leaves of the water lilies and the lotus. The small floating-leaved plants give a water garden the look of a pond created by nature.

Lotus

A magical member of the water lily family cultivated in ancient Egypt and the Orient, the exotic, heavily scented lotus makes a bridge between the floating leaves and flowers of the lilies and the upright foliage plants that frame the pond. First the lotus produces floating leaves, rather like big lily pads, then it lifts immense aerial leaves and magnificent blossoms upright and holds them an amazing 2 to 6 feet above the surface. Once you've seen a lotus come into bloom with flowers the diameter of a cantaloupe, you will never forget it. Even the seedpods are sculptural, and are treasured for use in dried flower arrangements. By hiding the sun and using up nutrients the algae need, lotus contribute to the clarity of the pond water.

Narrow-leaved Upright Marginals

The pond's marginal plants grow where water meets land, where soil plants give way to marshy plants and then to water-covered plants. The water garden needs uprights on at least one side to create a boundary and a background. Plants of various heights, textures, and colors are used, some for their flowers, others for the contrast provided by their narrow, elegant foliage. Irises are usually included; though their flowering period is brief, the swordlike foliage remains handsome for months. Cattails and the whispering, dancing ornamental grasses give movement and sound to the water garden. The marginals also help to remove some nutrients from the water.

Broad-leaved Upright Marginals

These marginal plants add broad leaves on upright stems to the water garden's background plantings. Many are bold natives of nature's watery places, and some are huge. Quite a few are planted primarily for their flowers; the bog lily, for instance, is one of summer's most beautiful bulb flowers. The tallest broad-leaved uprights sway a little when there's a breeze, joining the ornamental grasses in bringing motion and sound to the water garden.

Dwarf papyrus, a marginal. Plants that in nature grow at the water's edge are used as a backdrop in garden ponds.

The Fish

Their beauty, and the pleasure of knowing these gentle, color- ful little creatures, is only a part of their contribution to the water garden. Fish naturally dine on mosquitoes, insects, and the larvae that live underwater and at the surface, as well as on aphids and caterpillars. Their wastes provide nutrients that help sustain the aquatic plants. Plants consume carbon dioxide and release oxygen in sunlight, a function of photosynthesis. Fish take in that oxygen and release carbon dioxide. Rather like canaries in a coal mine, if fish aren't swimming around perkily in the pond, that's a clue to look for something wrong. For instance, the water pH — a measure of acidity/alkalinity — may need to be adjusted (see the recommendations in Chapter 3).

Snails and Other Helpers

The freshwater snail, a small black or brown-black scavenger, is the shining light of the pond's housekeeping department. In spring and summer you can spend hours watching the snails work the sides of the water garden, nibbling here and there. A mollusk with a house on its back, the snail grazes on dead leaves and plants and gobbles algae. The 1-inch-long black Japanese snail won't eat your ornamental plants, a forbearance not shown by all snails, and will not overpopulate the pond.

Another well-loved pond helper is the bullfrog, which makes those wonderful *nguu-nguu* sounds at night from its lily pad. Local native frogs may volunteer for mosquito patrol in your water garden, but most of the frogs in garden ponds are purchased as tadpoles. No matter how often you see it, the tadpole-to-frog transformation seems amazing. Not all make it to bullfroghood, but even the tadpoles do a fine job of clearing

'Attraction', a large water lily, has the undivided attention of this insect-eating member of the water garden family. (Photo by Anna M. L. Van Rooy)

up leftover fish food. Some people create a pond primarily because they want frogs, but remember that frogs are independent creatures, and they don't always stay. In rainy weather, especially, they're apt to go adventuring and not return.

2   Siting the Garden

Reflections. The beauty of the Japanese garden at the Brooklyn Botanic Garden is enhanced by a large expanse of open water. (Photo courtesy of Brooklyn Botanic Garden)

A WATER GARDEN can be a tub with a couple of Japanese fantails weaving languidly through the shadows of small lily pads. It can be a classic sheet of water and a fountain or a patch of wilderness designed to attract wildlife to a suburban backyard. What most gardeners want is a beautiful green and quiet place where they can contemplate their water lilies and enjoy the fish. Whatever its size and design, the water garden should be perfectly wedded to its particular site and your own way of living.

Stand at the windows of your house and consider potential sites. You'll want to see the pond all year round from your favorite places, not just in winter when the leaves are off the trees. Study possible sites from the porch or patio. Amble across the yard toward a site and see how the approach pleases you. Can the pond be placed so that it will mirror summer sunrises or fall moonsets? Before you decide on a size or a style, visualize the pond tied into the way the family uses the garden, and think about how it will fit with existing plantings and the contours of the land. If you are patient, the land itself will come up with suggestions. Rolling land with stony nooks and cran-

15

nies invites the idea of several small ponds that spill from one to the next. In a landscaped garden the inner curve of a flower border seems made to embrace a free-form pond. A small yard may be best enhanced, not by a tub or a kettle garden, as you might suppose, but by a relatively big water garden in surroundings given over entirely to setting it off.

Practical Considerations

In choosing a site, consider how it will meet the pond's few practical necessities. To bloom up to their potential, water lilies, lotus, and other aquatics need six or more hours of direct sun. Eight is better. The only water garden that actually needs some shade is a small tub or kettle garden: it will overheat in noonday sun, especially in hot regions. If your only pond site is sunlit for only four hours, it can be planted with shade-tolerant water lilies and marginal plants; to make the most of the sun, install a spray head that will catch rainbows in the light.

Good drainage of the area surrounding the pond is important. Avoid siting the pond in a low-lying area where puddles collect during wet periods and where the pond may be heaved each time the water table rises — with spring thaw, for instance, and after big storms. If the most suitable site is lower than the surrounding property, plan to grade the area around the site to avoid runoff water that will bring mud, grass, and weeds into the pond water and contaminate it with residues from chemically treated trees and grass, roofing, downspouts (fresh copper in particular), and petroleum from asphalt driveways. Or you can create diversion channels that will conduct the runoff water away from the pond. Avoid a site that collects blown debris and fallen leaves, and you probably won't need to empty and clean the pond in autumn.

Site the pond on ground that is level or can be leveled easily. An underlying rock ledge will have to be leveled with sand if you are using a preformed liner. A multilevel site presents no difficulty for a liner pond, but jagged edges of rock must be smoothed off to avoid tearing the liner. (Remember to use eye protectors when using a sledgehammer.) Make sure household electrical current and a ground-fault circuit interrupter are accessible for the electrical equipment.

You will need to add water to your pond now and then to compensate for evaporation, so place the water garden within reach of a hose. Not that a pond is a water guzzler: research at Boise State University in Idaho showed that keeping a pond full consumes half as much water as keeping a similar area of lawn growing. Lawn sprinklers have little effect on pond water unless their spray drips into the pond from foliage that's been treated with herbicides or pesticides. However, if your water supply is treated with chloramine, you must neutralize it because chloramine, like salt, remains indefinitely.

Consider how you are going to handle predators, notably raccoons. They are a genuine presence in cities and suburbs as well as in the country. Scrambling for fish, they'll upset the plantings and containers in your water garden, not to mention the fish. And raccoons love *escargots au naturel*; they'll bring the snails right up out of the pond, pick the meat out, and leave the shells in a row along the coping.

A first line of defense where predators are plentiful is to make the sides of the pond nearly vertical. Small, furry creatures find fishing more hazardous when the level of the water is well below the pond ledge, out of paw's reach. Another way to protect fish from predators is to place a pile of weathered cinderblocks or smooth stones in the pond to create a safe haven where the fish can hide. Placing screens across the pond at night is one solution to nocturnal raids, but that is a chore and they are unattractive. A custom-made grid of fencing placed 6 to 12 inches under the surface of the water allows fish to dive to safety below the reach of the raccoons' sharp claws. A low-voltage electric fence installed at a distance from the pond greater than the length of the predator's body can be effective. After an encounter or two, the offender will probably respect the fence even if the power is off. A dog may keep predators away from the pond. If all else fails, keep less colorful fish, or decide to have a pond for wildlife, and invite your visitors to join the family. Some experts say that you can keep colorful fish even if you have visiting raccoons if the pond is built with nearly vertical walls and without a shelf for marginal plants.

Selecting a Water Garden

As long as it gets six hours of sun, the water garden can be contained in almost anything, even a 16-quart plastic pan just big enough for a plant with miniature floating leaves. An old oak whiskey barrel, halved, aged enough to be odorless, and lined to keep out exudates, can become a water garden full of character. It is large enough to contain a small floating-leaved plant and an upright marginal plant.

Aquatic suppliers offer a variety of small water gardens, including tubs 18 to 28 inches across by 12 to 18 inches deep; decorative pans 28 inches in diameter and 13½ inches deep; and kettles, about 3 feet in diameter and 18 inches deep. These accommodate the requisite submerged plants and beautiful little groupings of ornamental aquatics — for instance, the small tropical water lily 'Dauben' with variegated sweet flag for vertical accent and frills of parrot's feather cascading over the

Even a small tub can accommodate variegated canna, a small tropical lily, and parrot's feather, an ornamental species of myriophyllum that grows on the surface of the water and helps keep it clear. Cranes and potted garden plants screen the container. (Photo by Elvin McDonald)

edge. You should have two or three fish, each 2 to 3 inches long, for mosquito control, and two snails. For a tub garden a small pump isn't essential, but it is helpful. When the level of oxygen is low (especially during hot, muggy weather, electrical storms, or periods of algae bloom), the oxygenating effect of recirculated water can save your fish. The sound of water gurgling into even a small pond is pleasing.

More than 90 percent of new backyard ponds are lined with a sheet of flexible rubber, fish-grade PVC (polyvinyl chloride), or preformed fiberglass or plastic. These installations are so simple that most owners put together the whole system with products sold at large garden centers or through mail order specialists.

Preformed fiberglass ponds are a good choice for a small pond — 4 by 6 feet or a little larger. That size will hold two water lilies, a small floating-leaved plant, one or two upright plants, and the fish and snails.

For larger ponds, however, most people choose a pre-cut or custom-cut flexible liner because it is significantly less expensive than a preformed pond. A preformed pond is about four times as expensive as a liner that makes the same size pond. A preformed pond must have an excavation dug to its shape, while a liner can be adapted to almost any shape you choose. The thicker the rubber or PVC, the more it will cost and the longer it will last. A 20-mil-thick PVC liner might need to be replaced in seven to ten years, while a 32-mil PVC liner has a life expectancy of fifteen to twenty years. The UV (ultra-violet) stabilized rubber liners are similar in cost to those made of PVC, and they will withstand the effects of hot sun for up to thirty years. Liners with geotextile backing bonded to them usually are sold with a guarantee that they will last your life-time. With a geotextile backing you don't need a protective underlayment, which saves some steps in the installation pro-cess described later in the chapter.

The average small pond is 15 to 30 inches deep, and this suits the fish as well as the plants. A pond shallower than 15 inches is less satisfactory for water lilies and lotus and is quick to cloud with algae stimulated by the buildup of heat. In cold climates, Zone 4 and colder, fish will survive the winter in better shape in ponds that are 30 to 48 inches deep and equipped with a de-icer. Depths greater than that may present a safety hazard. Some localities require fencing for ponds over 24 or 30 inches deep. Check with local authorities before you excavate.

The popular pond dimensions are from 10 by 10 to 10 by 15 feet — the size of a living room rug — with surfaces of 100 to 150 square feet and capacities of 1,000 to 2,000 gallons of water, depending on the surface area, slope, use of shelves, and depth. Such a pond will fit in almost any yard and can accommodate a lovely collection of diverse aquatic plants, including at least five water lilies, one lotus, and twenty-four floating and marginal plants — say eight types, with three of each kind in each of eight containers. An attractive combination is floating-heart and water clover, which have small floating leaves, and irises, pickerel rush, cattails, equisetum (horsetail), and two other upright marginals.

A 10-by-10-foot pond is easier to maintain than a flower border half that size. It is also easier to maintain than a very small pond. In a larger pond the loss of two or three goldfish doesn't affect the overall balance, but in a tub garden that could be the entire goldfish population.

Ferns and a backdrop of upright marginal plants frame a small liner pond tucked into a corner of a fenced backyard. The huge leaves in the background are taro, Colocasia esculenta. *(Photo by Kenneth Molacek)*

Pond Designs

Once you have chosen a site, consider how you will plant the surroundings to make the pond look as though it belongs. The setting — the background — dictates the style of the pond design.

To make a tub garden or a barrel look at home, surround it closely with plants in harmony with nearby garden areas. Set the plants at different heights, as they would be found in nature, and choose plants that both contrast with and complement one or two small, refined marginals growing in the pond.

For a formal pond, choose a symmetrical shape, perhaps an oval or a long rectangle, and provide it with a symmetrical background. Matched plantings on either side of a higher or lower central point give a pond a formal aspect. Use background plants associated with formal landscapes, such as boxwood and roses. Trimmed hedges and topiaries achieve instant formality for their surroundings. Have the water return to the pond through a piece of classical statuary — a human figure, fish, flowers, or frogs, for instance.

Choose a high-style design if you want to play. A Japanese garden invites a small, arched red bridge over a narrow portion of the water garden. A towering fountain of water makes a very dramatic statement in a large landscape.

A naturalized pond calls for an asymmetrical shape, and the plants in the garden nearby should not all be matched and paired. Several good-sized clumps of irises balanced by one young Japanese maple is more natural and less formal than a pair of matched Japanese maples flanking the water garden. Use plants that naturally grow near water — water-loving reeds and grasses, shrubs such as pussy willow, clethra, red osier dogwood, winterberry, sweetspire, spicebush, and

The cement basin and stonework here are typical of British water gardens. In North America winter's repeated freezing and thawing tend to heave and crack all but the most substantial — and costly — masonry ponds. (Photo by Bill Heritage.)

sweet elder, and trees such as alder, serviceberry, river birch, American hornbeam, wild olive, sweet gum, Austrian pine, and bald cypress. (But avoid planting trees or shrubs where the leaves will be swept into the pond come fall.) The water lilies and lotus require lots of sun, but the waterfall can be partially shaded, and there you can plant a few lovely ferns and green mosses.

A Few Do's and a Don't

Use a black pond liner. Black liners give the water a more natural look than marine blue or any other color because the surface of most small natural bodies of water appears black. Black mirrors the sky and the water lilies and other plants and also shows off the glinting colors of the fish. Match the pond pump and other submerged equipment to the liner color so that they become invisible.

To enhance the color of the flowers in the pond and to tie the design of the water garden into the surrounding landscaping, repeat the pond flower colors in the plants growing around the pond.

Give careful thought to your choice of stones for the coping, for a waterfall, and for lining a watercourse. Large flat stones that match the rock outcroppings in your area will look best, but keep the stones in scale with the size of the pond. Study nature and imitate it. Don't place stones in positions you don't see in nature.

Where space is at a premium, design the pond into the major landscape feature. For instance, a patch of water looks surprisingly right set up against a wall or fence edging a townhouse lot.

Backyard Wildlife

Water gardens attract local wildlife, for water is as essential to animals as it is to us. Site the pond where you can enjoy watching your flying or furred friends from several positions without disturbing the guests, and make the area safe and comfortable for them. A pump and a small waterfall are assets for a wildlife pond, but filters may not be. Very clear water makes the fish more visible to furred and feathered fishermen. Native minnows (where permitted) and small goldfish are better choices for a wildlife pond than the gorgeous koi, which tend to end up as meals for your guests, especially raccoons.

The pond's location and size govern the creatures that will come to it. Small urban ponds attract songbirds, butterflies, and dragonflies, and for these a body of water 2 by 3 feet is generous. For a frog, that's minimal space. In the suburbs or the country a secluded pond of 10 by 10 feet or larger may attract deer, foxes, raccoons, possums, and other small animals, as well as small songbirds and game birds.

Domestic cats are not great fishermen, but experts say that on land they are two or three times as effective at the hunt as lions and tigers in the wild. If you want birds to come down to a pond in cat territory, they will need a high, safe observation post and retreat 6 to 8 feet from the pond. The perch can be a tree or thick shrubbery in which small birds can hide from hawks and other predators. Birds need a clear flight path to the pond, for they all tend to follow the same approach pattern into a water area. Generally, they fly first to a high-up faraway branch, then come in closer to check out the territory, and finally fly down to the water. An ideal landing site is a broad, flat stone, perhaps in the middle of the pond, that gently rises from the water, making a sloping platform for drinking and bathing. Birds are attracted by plants with berries and those that provide nesting materials, such as grasses, bark-shedding trees, twiggy shrubs, thistles, and milkweed.

Installing the Pond

A home water garden can be installed in one weekend by two people. Neighbors are sure to become spectators, and they can be helpful when it's time to set the liner or the preformed pond

1. Anstace and Larry Esmonde-White, left and center, and Richard Koogle measure a pond planned for the inside curve of a flowering border, well away from any leaf-shedding trees. (All photos by George L. Thomas III)

into the excavation. The photos that follow were taken when Richard Koogle, of Lilypons Water Gardens, demonstrated the installation of a free-form PVC liner pond at Buckeystown, Maryland, for Anstace and Larry Esmonde-White, hosts of the PBS television show "From a Country Garden."

A shelf cut into the sides of the pond is widely used in Britain for marginal plants, and in the sequence that follows we show how to create a pond with a shelf. Most American water gardeners prefer straight sides, which are something of a deterrent to predators and allow more space for water. Also, you can create more interesting designs with the marginal plants by moving them around the pond floor and placing them on raised pots, clean bricks, or weathered cinderblocks than by lining them up on a shelf.

The instructions are for a liner that does not have its own geotextile underlayment. A liner that has its own underlayment is easier to work with.

2. The pond has been excavated to 24 inches, with a shelf for marginal plants. The sod has been peeled back from the pond edge along one side.

Step 1. Flexible liner pond

To calculate the size of the liner for your pond, outline the site with a garden hose or string and decide on a depth between 15 and 30 inches. To determine the width of the liner you will need, measure and add the maximum width of the pond (measured at a 90-degree angle to the maximum length) to twice the depth (for the sides), then add 2 feet for the edging. To determine the length of liner needed, add the maximum length of the pond to twice the depth and add 2 feet for the edging. (An experienced installer may add less than 2 feet for the edges.) If you are planning a rectangular or square pond, use stakes and a carpenter's square to get the angles exactly right. To outline a circular pond, use a string tied to a central stake. Choosing a compact shape allows you to have a larger pond with less liner material cut off. If your earth is rocky and you are not sure whether you will be able to excavate the

3. A board and a carpenter's level are used to make sure that the edge is even all around.

shape you want, make the excavation first, then measure for the size liner you need.

Step 1. Preformed pond

Outline the site for a preformed pond by tracing around the top edge (have the pond right side up) to determine the digging area. Use sand to line and level the bottom of the excavation.

Step 2. Liner pond

If you plan to have a coping around the pond that you can stand on, you must prepare the base for it at this point. Before excavating the pond, dig a trench 12 inches wide and 8 inches deep (deeper in Zones 2–6, shallower in Zones 8–10) around the perimeter. Drive wooden pegs into the center of the trench at 1- to 2-foot intervals, keeping the tops of the pegs level with the top of the trench. Pour

4. Sand lines the floor of the excavation, and geotextile material cushion the sides.

a premixed concrete (mix with water according to the instructions on the bag) into the trench up to the tops of the pegs, smoothing and leveling the concrete with a trowel. Allow it to set for twenty-four hours, then continue with the instructions for excavating the pond. The interior wall of the concrete base becomes part of the wall of the excavation.

Excavate the site to the pond depth you have decided on. Outline an area in the center of the pond floor about 18 inches across, and dig that about an inch deeper. (When you drain the pond for cleaning, the fish will gather in this depression, allowing you to net them quickly for transfer to a holding tank.) Pile all the excavated soil on a tarpaulin away from the side of the pond. Slope the sides at a 75-degree angle, as measured from a line across the top of the excavation to the slope of the side. If the site has very loose sandy soil, angle the sides closer to 45 degrees to keep

5. *Smoothing the unfolded liner: the only requirement is plenty of patience.*

them from caving in. Clay soil will allow you to have 90-degree sides, which may help to discourage some predators.

If desired, leave a ledge or shelf all or partway around the excavation to hold the marginal plants. The shelf should be 9 to 15 inches deep and wide, proportioned to the size of the pond, the height of your soil containers, and the marginal plants it is to accommodate. If there are lots of raccoons in the area, plan to raise your marginal plants to the desired height on upended pots, clean bricks, or weathered cinderblocks rather than on a shelf. Slope the sides of the shelf inward at a 75-degree angle, keeping the bottom as uniformly level as possible.

Step 2. Preformed pond

Prepare coping and excavate as above, following the shape of the preformed water garden. Arrange 1 to 2 inches of sand on the bottom of the excavation so that the top of the pond is level.

6. *After the pond is filled, the liner is nailed in place.*

Step 3. Liner and preformed pond

It is very important that the top edge of the excavation be level all around to within ¼ inch so you don't have any water spillage. Place a 2-by-4-inch board across the center of the excavation and check the level with a carpenter's level at various points. Flatten any high spots around the rim. Use sand, tamped down, to raise areas of the edge up to 2 inches if necessary; use cinderblocks, bricks, slate, or treated wood covered with sand to raise areas more than 2 inches. It's better to shave high spots than to fill low spots, as long as this doesn't drop the edge of the pond below the level of the surrounding terrain.

Step 4. Liner and preformed pond

Outline a rim 12 to 15 inches wide all around the pond and remove the sod to make space for the coping stones or other edging material. If you plan to have grass growing right down to the edge of the pond to create a natural look, make

7. The coping stones are positioned after the sod has been replaced.

shallow 24-inch-long cuts in the sod every 10 inches. Gently roll the sod back and keep it moist as you continue with the installation. Recheck the levels, and go over the entire area carefully to remove sharp stones and roots.

For a liner pond, add 1 inch of damp sand to the bottom of the excavation to cushion and protect the liner. Cover the sides of the excavation with geotextile underlayment or old carpet underlayment. If the liner has its own geotextile underlayment, this step is omitted.

Step 5. Liner pond

This part of the project requires muscle. You can figure out in advance how much help you will need by calculating the weight of the liner. Every 100 square feet of 20-mil PVC weighs 14 to 15 pounds; of 32-mil PVC, 24 pounds; of 45-mil EPDM rubber, 30 pounds; and of 60-mil GeoPond, 20 pounds.

8. The new water garden is finished. In a few weeks the lawn will begin to green, and garden plants will soften the pond's raw edge.

Unfold the liner and allow it to warm in the sun briefly until it is flexible and easy to work with. Don't leave it on grass in the hot sun for more than a few minutes because the heat buildup will quickly kill the grass. Carefully lift the liner and spread it over the pond and the edges. If you find the liner too heavy to lift easily after it has been unfolded, refold it, place it in the center of the excavation, and unfold it from there. Weight the edges down with smooth stones or bricks to prevent the wind from blowing the liner into the excavation. Recheck the level.

Step 5. Preformed pond

Set the fiberglass form in the excavation so that the rim is just above ground level. Recheck the level of the rim and mark areas that need adjusting to level the pond. Remove the pond and use a rake to level the sand on the excavation floor. Repeat the process until the pool edges are level to within ¼ inch.

Step 6. Liner pond

Fill the pond with water to within an inch of the top. Cut off the surplus liner with a pair of large, sharp scissors or a razor-sharp knife, leaving a flap 6 to 12 inches wide around the entire pond. Use 4- to 6-inch nails to nail the liner into the ground 4 to 10 inches from the pond edge to keep it in place when you lay the coping stones around the pond.

Step 6. Preformed pond

Begin filling the pond, and as the water level rises, pack sand or soil behind the sides to keep the pressure on the fiberglass walls the same inside and outside.

Step 7. Liner and preformed pond

If you have poured a 12-inch-deep concrete base (see Step 1), you will be able to walk on the coping around the pond. If not, the stones will be ornamental. In either case, lay out the coping stones so you can arrange them in the best way. Place strips of metal lath (from a building supply store) over the liner flap, then place the stones in the desired pattern around the pond. For mortar, use either a premixed mortar with sand or, better, use one part (by volume) Portland cement and two parts sand, thoroughly mixed dry. Slowly add water to achieve a plasticlike consistency — more fluid than putty but not so liquid as to flow through your fingers. Remove one stone at a time and smooth the mortar onto the metal lath with a trowel. Then replace the stone and tap it into position with a rubber hammer. The stones should

Coping stones hide the upper edge of the pond liner amd protect it from the damaging ultraviolet rays of the sun.

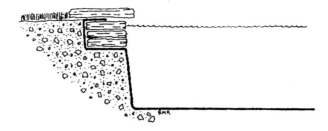

extend 1 to 2 inches over the pond to protect the liner from the sun's destructive ultraviolet rays. The coping stones will look more natural if you use very little mortar between them. Check the level of the stones often as you work.

When the coping is complete, drain the pond, using the pump and its tubing, or siphon off the water with a hose. Remove any excess mortar on the coping, and clean the pond of droppings. Then refill the pond with fresh water. Once the mortar in the coping is dry (twenty-four hours), clean it with a stiff brush and a mixture of one part ordinary vinegar to five parts water; this will ensure that the lime in the mortar will not kill the fish. Rinse the area thoroughly. Monitor the pH of the pond water to see if it is affected by the alkalinity of the mortar, particularly after the first couple of rains.

The pond is now ready for plants, but the goldfish and other small creatures will have to wait another week or two before they can move in.

3 🐚 Clear, Beautiful Water

Water lilies and daylilies are mirrored in the quiet waters below a gentle 3-foot waterfall, high enough to screen a pond filter. Pickerel rush and variegated sweet flag frame the garden. (Photo by Stephen H. Smith)

WATER IS THE POND'S MAGIC, the cradle that gently rocks the lily pads and nourishes life, a mirror for sunrises and moonsets. Reflecting the sky, bouncing raindrops, gurgling up through a bubbler, the color and the mood of the water are an ever-changing delight.

The one constant factor in a pond is the growth of algae in warm weather. It's important to your enjoyment to understand early on that the crystal-clear water of a newly filled pond isn't the only optimum condition. Once it's been dechlorinated,* a little green comes into every water garden; that is, there's some algae in every healthy pond. Greenwater algae are microscopic single-cell plants, generally water-dwelling, with a very simple structure. Each cell contains chlorophyll and multiplies by division. Algae need nitrogen and sunlight to grow. Green water doesn't harm the fish, the birds, or the butterflies — actually, fish can thrive in water so green you can barely see your hand a foot down. Once you know one alga from another,

---

* We use the term to describe removing from the pond water chlorine and other chlorine-based chemicals, notably chloramine and chlorine dioxide.

why they're there and what they do, good and bad, you'll have more faith in the water garden's ability to keep itself beautiful.

Algae

The worst attack of green, or green-brown, algae a pond faces is the murky period that occurs after you first fill and dechlorinate the pond. It begins within a week and grows more dense by the day. In a pond started in spring, the condition usually ends in six to eight weeks, especially if the pond includes the requisite number of submerged plants and one of the biological filters described in the next chapter. A well-stocked pond begun in hot weather occasionally stays murky for more than eight weeks. Happily, once the water clears up, it should stay clear except for a brief murky period each spring. Algae respond more quickly to the warmth of spring than do the other plants competing with it for nutrients. In an established water garden, the algal head start begins a week or two after warm weather wakens the pond and lasts a few weeks. Then the submerged plants, water lilies, and other ornamentals begin to outstrip the algae in taking up nutrients, and the greenwater algae lose out.

In a well-balanced pond, some algae are always present, and they are beneficial. Algae are one of nature's contributions to the ecosystem you have put together. Borne on the wind by invisible spores, algae grow wherever they find light, warmth, nutrients, and water. In a water garden there are three main types: a filamentous type, a surface-floating type, and the suspended unicellular greenwater algae. The filamentous type has two forms, one of which is beneficial. It mosses the sides of the pond with deep green filaments and fuzzes plant stems and snail shells, making the pond look more natural. A certain amount is present even in ponds with crystal-clear water. The other form occurs in long suspended strings that may, if not physically removed, be sucked in by your pump and clog it. The floating alga is not common in American water gardens, but in England, where it is known as blanketweed, it is a pest usually disposed of by applying algicide or by netting it or overflowing it out of the pond. Gardeners can get rid of blanketweed simply by raising the water level and floating it off the surface with the aid of a broom or a fishnet.

The third type, unicellular algae, is the principal maker of murk. Some is visible and some invisible to the naked eye, but it gives the pond a green or green-brown cast. A small amount of the greenish tinge is welcomed by most pond keepers. It brings a hint of mystery to the water and masks the submerged pots in which the aquatic plants grow without hiding the flashing colors of the ornamental fish.

Like other green plants, algae make major contributions to the pond. The sequence of their nitrogen cycle has a little of the rhyme and rhythm of "The House That Jack Built," or the song about the thigh bone connected to the hip bone:

Fish food, ingested, is followed by
fish waste, which releases
ammonia, a suffocating gas, which
bacteria, living under mosslike algae on the pool sides, transform into
nitrites, which other
bacteria, beneath the mossy algae, transform into
nitrates, a fertilizer, which is grabbed by the
submerged and ornamental plants, and which feeds the
algae, which greens the water, and which
fish eat in small quantities.

As this tropical water garden demonstrates, green water can be beautiful and fish can thrive in it. Cattail is used as a linear accent plant. (Photo by Elvin McDonald)

Simple Solutions to Unwelcome Abundance

However beneficial some algae can be, clear water and feeding the fish are part of the owner's pleasure, and an excess of the green-brown stuff in a new pond is viewed with limited joy, and even the urge to kill. After two or three weeks in which the water gets increasingly murky, you may be tempted to drain the pond, remove the plants, the fish, and the scavengers and start over with crystal-clear water. This is exactly the wrong thing to do. A new pond *must* go through those start-up murky green-water blues until it develops the balance that will clear it. If the green persists beyond the predictable period, there are some simple, natural remedies.

Two frequent causes of excess suspended algae in ponds new and old are an overabundance of nutrients from overfeeding the fish and too many fish for the size of the pond. If you have been feeding the fish, stop for a week or two. In a pond well stocked with plants, especially submerged plants, this may solve the problem. You will miss the daily exchange, but suspending the feeding will encourage the fish to forage more diligently. The pond is well able to feed them, and the beneficial algae will survive perfectly well.

The submerged plants are very efficient feeders; they take up the nitrates as fast as the bacteria can release them if you have enough plants. If your pond is more heavily stocked with fish than is suggested in the magic formula given in Chapter 5, you will need more submerged plants to keep up with the fish waste. You could also give away some of the fish or get a filter, preferably a biological filter, to deal with the problem. With enough submerged plants, pond water can be almost crystal clear. If a murky condition persists, check the position of the submerged plants. The suspended algae may be blocking their light, so raise the containers closer to the surface until you are sure they are getting direct sun. When the pond clears, return the submerged grasses to their regular depth.

If you continue to have murky water, refigure the proportions of submerged plants, snails, and floating plants you have decided on (see the formula in Chapter 5). Often a small change in the proportions of these elements or a decrease in the number of fish will result in moderately clear water.

Black Dye to the Rescue
Gardeners who are very eager to have a pond look algae-free and those who dislike even a little green in the water can solve their problem instantly by adding a black dye specially formulated for water gardens. This is the product that gives the National Aquatic Gardens at the U.S. National Arboretum in Washington, D.C., the velvety black look of a very deep body of water. Many outstanding water gardens, such as those at

Longwood Gardens, in Kennett Square, Pennsylvania, rely on the dye to hide the plant containers. The dye has no known bad side effects. You will be able to see only 6 to 12 inches down, depending on the amount of dye you use. But the inky surface mirrors the sky beautifully, and against its midnight black the water lilies snap bright green, and the glistening gold, white, and orange fish seem to float in and out of a mysterious deep.

The label on the dye container will explain how much to use; the amount does not depend on water temperature. As with food seasoning, you may use more or less than the suggested amount. After you've used the dye once or twice, you'll know how much you want to put in. It's safe for pets and wildlife, although some individual creatures may be allergic to the dye, just as some people are allergic to milk or eggs. The dye doesn't kill the algae, it simply spares you the sight of it. As long as you can clearly see the tops of the submerged plants, enough sunlight is getting through to supply the needs of the beneficial algae and other plants.

Algicides — Maybe

Approved algicides, like the sprays used on garden aphids, offer a quick solution if nature's way fails to satisfy your idea of how the pond should look. Most pond owners use an algicide at one time or another to improve the appearance of the water. Many use it when the pond goes into its green-water phase in spring. But for most of the year the submerged plants and other recommended elements will keep the pond in balance and the water clear and beautiful. If you want extra insurance against green water, invest in a filter and recirculating pump. The less you depend on algicides, the better.

At Longwood Gardens, as at many public water gardens, a benign black dye is added to the lily ponds to create the illusion of depth and to mask coins tossed by wishful visitors. (Photo by L. Albee, Longwood Gardens)

Before you buy an algicide, study the label and make sure your choice is safe for everything in your pond. Some algicides that do not harm fish may severely stress or kill water lilies and other aquatic plants. Other algicides are safe for plants; some are safe for goldfish but not for koi, golden orfe, or local game fish such as trout, bass, or bluegills.

Never use more of an algicide than the label suggests for a pond containing fish and plants. Apply it between eight and ten in the morning, when the oxygen content of the water is rising. When used as directed, an algicide will kill the undesirable algae promptly; the algae growing on the sides of the pond tend to be more resistant and usually survive. As the organic matter decomposes, it often uses up oxygen faster than the water can absorb it from the air. You'll know you have an acute shortage of oxygen if the fish come to the surface to gulp air. You can avoid this problem by turning on your recirculating pump; as it pushes water over a waterfall or through statuary or a bubbler, oxygen is added to the water.

Oxygen and Air Pumps

An acute oxygen shortage is quickly relieved by an air pump. This is a simple, lightweight, inexpensive accessory that you will be very glad you have on the rare occasions when it is needed. For instance, if you put a lot of fish in a small holding tank while the pond is being cleaned, they may rapidly consume all the oxygen. Or the quality of the water in the pond may be poor in high heat or muggy weather, or during and right after an electrical storm. To correct the problem, use the air pump to force air, which is 20 percent oxygen, into the water and run it until the fish are back below the surface swimming normally.

pH and All That

Many plants thrive in soil that is fairly acid, pH 5.5 to 6.5, but the ideal reading for water gardens is neutral, pH 7.0. Fluctuations between 6.5 and 7.5 are normal, but anything beyond that range calls for observation and possible correction. You should monitor conditions outside of the 6.5–7.5 range but treat only if the pH is below 6 or above 8. Check with a pH tester before you put fish or other creatures into a newly filled and dechlorinated pond. Take pH readings for three days running, around eight in the morning when the water is nearest neutral. A week or so after putting the fish into the water, run another series of tests. If you've had trouble with the pH, repeat the tests after adding new plants or new fish. Otherwise, test monthly and whenever the fish become lethargic but show no signs of disease.

Fish are both a warning system and a potential cause of water problems. Too many fish or too much fish food results in more ammonia in the water than the plants can absorb; that may be accompanied by a pH that rises toward 8.0 or even 9.0. The solution is to cut back on fish food and correct the condition with a pH reducer such as AlkaMinus. If the water is too acid, AlkaPlus or ordinary baking soda will sweeten it. For each 100 gallons of water, add 1 teaspoonful of soda each day until the pH test is satisfactory.

Most water gardeners don't have pH problems, but to be on the safe side you should check it now and then. If you try to adjust the pH to 7.0 every day you are more likely to have difficulties. Fish and plants that have adapted to a particular level of acidity or alkilinity may suffer if you make a sudden and significant change. Normal rain will not have a negative effect unless there is runoff from chemically treated

White lilies float on velvety black water. The plant resting on the surface, left, is anacharis, one of the submerged plants that have a vital part in keeping pond water clear. (Photo by Emerson Freese)

trees or grass. Nature does a pretty good job of maintaining the correct pH for your pond.

Dechlorinating

Fish and the other creatures in your pond cannot thrive, and may even die, in water containing chlorine or one of the other products used to treat drinking water. You can wait for chlorine to escape from the water before you stock it initially. But after cleaning or topping off the pond, you will have to use a dechlorinating agent. If you add 10 percent of the volume of water in the pond — for instance, if your 20-inch-deep pond is down 2 inches — add 10 percent of the dechlorinator you put into the pond when you first filled it. Find out from your local public water department which chlorinating product is used in your water and use only a dechlorinating agent specifically designed for that product. Follow the label instructions exactly.

Chlorine is the most common chemical used to treat drinking water. The amount of chlorine used in city drinking water won't bother plants, but it can kill fish within hours or even minutes. In an open-air pond, chlorine escapes in two or three days, and after that it poses no threat to the fish. The much higher concentration of chlorine used in swimming pools would affect plants adversely and of course would kill the fish.

Chloramine is far less commonly used to treat drinking water, but its use is increasing. Though harmless to plants in the quantities used in drinking water, in several weeks chloramine will kill fish. *Chloramine does not naturally escape from the water.* It must always be neutralized chemically if you plan to have fish in your pond. Aquatic nurseries and pet shops that sell fish should know whether local water supplies are treated with chloramine and should carry products for neutralizing it.

Chlorine dioxide, which is not used in many places, is different from either chlorine or chloramine and requires special treatment. The simplest solution is to apply a double dose of the chemicals that dissipate ordinary chlorine. Some water departments switch back and forth between chlorine and chlorine dioxide. In that case you should find out which product is being used each time you treat the water.

Taking Pond Measurements: Surface Size and Gallons

Before you can consider how many plants and fish your pond should have, you need to establish its surface area and the number of gallons of water it will hold. It is easy to calculate the size of even a kidney-shaped or free-form pond by bending the form in your imagination into a square, rectangle, or circle or a combination of those shapes. Once you have figured out your pond's surface area and capacity in gallons, record the information in a log book or garden diary. You will need to refer to these figures at various times.

To calculate the number of *square feet* on the surface of a rectangular pond, multiply the length (in feet) times the width (in feet):

length × width = square feet of surface

If the pond is circular, multiply 3.14 times half the diameter times half the diameter (in feet):

3.14 (½ diameter × ½ diameter) = square feet of surface

To calculate the number of *cubic feet* in a rectangular pond, multiply the length (in feet) times the width (in feet) times the depth (in feet):

length × width × depth = volume in cubic feet

For a circular pond, multiply 3.14 times ½ the diameter times ½ the diameter times the depth (all measurements in feet):

3.14 × (½ diameter × ½ diameter) × depth = volume in cubic feet

To calculate the number of *gallons* of water in your pond, multiply the number of cubic feet times 7.5 gallons. (There are 7.5 gallons of water per cubic foot.)

cubic feet × 7.5 gallons = capacity in gallons

4 🐚 Pumps, Filters, and the Sounds of Water

A statue in the classical manner lends grace and formality to a pond. Aerating the water improves the quality of life for the fish.

*T*HE SOUND OF WATER bubbling up, rushing through stones, cascading into the pond — these musical aspects of a well-endowed water garden are powered by a submersible electric recirculating pump. While the effect is enchanting, the practical purpose of the pump is to improve the quality of the water. Set a few inches above the bottom of the pond where the level of oxygen is lowest, the pump's first job usually is to push or pull the water through a filter that removes suspended algae, fish food, and waste. Then it forces the water through tubing up into a bubbler, piped statue, or fountain or to a waterfall or watercourse, which returns it to the pond by gravity. The size of the pond and the height of the water feature dictate the choice and cost of the pump. It is possible to have a pond without a pump or to have a pump without a filter. Filtering isn't required in a properly stocked, well-balanced pond, but owners of water gardens generally invest in both a pump and a filter. If your pond includes fish, and especially the beautiful and seemingly ever-hungry koi, a pump and filter provide strong insurance against algae buildup.

The pump and filter are not usually part of the pond installation, so they can be added after the pond has been completed if you decide you do want this equipment.

Filters

Some small filters come equipped with a pump, and filter manufacturers indicate the pond size and pump rating for their product. The two common types of filter are mechanical filters and biological filters.

Mechanical Filters

A mechanical filter is the simpler of the two types to install and the less expensive, but it needs the most attention. The pump pulls water through a pad or wrap of material that traps suspended particles. Or the pump may force water into a sealed tank that is usually outside of the pond, where the filter may be removed and cleaned more easily. Some mechanical filters need cleaning twice daily during hot weather, every three to five days at other times.

Cleaning is simple — just hose off the filter pad or wrap in a place where the rinse water won't go back into the pond. Filters are generally 13 to 20 inches long and are light enough to lift easily. It is important to clean the filter before it becomes clogged, for the pump may suffer damage if not enough water is passing through it. If less than the normal amount of water is flowing through the bubbler, statue, fountain, or waterfall, check the filter. However, a reduced flow of water can also be caused by a clogged volute in the pump or by tubing that is constricted or needs cleaning.

To be effective, a mechanical filter requires a pump that can recirculate all the water in the pond at least once every two hours. For a pond holding 300 gallons of water or less, a small, inexpensive pump-filter combination is suitable. One popular model has enough power to recirculate 170 gallons of water an hour and push it through tubing to a waterfall that flows back into the pond. In two hours it can pump 340 gallons of water, more than enough for filtering a pond this size. It may require cleaning daily when the water temperature is over 65 or 70 degrees.

Equally suitable for a small pond is the similar but more powerful tube type of mechanical filter. This filter has a Velcro-fastened wrap and is connected by tubing to a small pump. It is offered in three different sizes to handle the water volume of various typical ponds. The pump, sold separately, should be chosen according to the size of the pond and the distance you want to lift or move the water. The combination of pump and tube filter can recirculate up to 2,000 gallons of water in two hours. The filter wrap will need cleaning every one to five days during the growing season.

For larger ponds, there are filter and pump combinations capable of handling up to 4,000 gallons of water an hour. That is the capacity of a water garden 16 feet wide by 24 feet long, as large as a fair-sized living room. Typically, the pump pushes water up to the filter unit, which releases it over a waterfall and then returns it to the pond. The filter must be rinsed every two to seven days in summer.

Biological Filters

A biological filter is a gravel-filled tank typically 30 to 45 inches high that is installed outside the pond and usually screened by a waterfall, plantings, or decorative fencing. If made of fiberglass, the system will last indefinitely. Though more expensive initially, it is more interesting and more sophisticated than a mechanical filter. Even more meaningful to the pond owner is the glorious fact that a biological filter needs attention only one to four times a month, not daily. Also, the pump used with a biological filter is less costly and uses less electricity because the water is recirculated once every four to six hours rather than every two hours as for a mechanical filter. The slower filtering action keeps the water clear just about all the time, and does it at a lower energy cost. Biological filters are manufactured in sizes that handle from 200 to 2,000 gallons of water or more. Units can be combined for larger ponds.

The cleansing action in a biological filter is nature's own; the filtering is done by gravel and bacteria that colonize the gravel. The most efficient system has an aeration tower, a cylinder that stands a foot or more above the filter tank and reaches to its bottom. The pump pushes the water through rigid PVC tubing from the pond to the top of the aeration tower, where it splashes down, absorbing oxygen as it falls, to the bottom of the tank. From there it rises through a layer of coarse gravel, then through a layer of finer gravel in the top half of the tank. The gravel traps debris. As the water rises, it is cleansed by bacteria in the nooks and crannies of the gravel. These bacteria require oxygen — that's why an aeration tower is more efficient. Because there is more oxygen in the water, more bacteria thrive. By the time the water reaches the top of the tank, it is clear. The top layer of gravel is covered by several inches of water and may be planted with submerged plants like *Myriophyllum* or anacharis or some of the small floating-leaved plants that "polish" the water by gobbling nitrates the bacteria derive from ammonia. The water then flows over a waterfall or into tubing that carries it back into the pond.

The best biological filters allow you to stop the pump, open a valve, and let the water in the filter drain over nearby garden plants. Doing this one to four times a month will encourage phenomenal growth in your garden! Fish waste is a great fertilizer. In warm weather and in frost-free regions the filter may need draining more often, especially if you have a lot of fish. A biological filter should be thoroughly cleaned once a year, during the coolest part of winter in frost-free regions and at the end of the growing season in the cooler zones.

The bacteria that clean the water in a biological filter are the same as those that grow beneath the beneficial dark green mosslike algae around the sides of a pond. They need a few weeks to become established; you can jump-start a new biological filter system by pouring in canned bacteria bought from an aquatic plant specialist.

Pumps

The cost of a pump is quite modest, so be sure to buy one that is large enough for your needs. The pump's rated capacity is the maximum rate for that piece of equipment. A pump with more than the minimum capacity required for your pond size can do the job, and one with less than that cannot. If the pump has more than the minimum power, it will be able to push water through the system at the correct rate even when there is some debris covering the intake screen. This gives you a little more time before you have to clean out the screen. If necessary, the flow of water out of the pump can be slowed either by adding a restrictive clamp to the discharge tubing or by attaching the pump to a restrictive fountainhead or piece of statuary.

It is easy to install a little submersible pump yourself. Place the pump on clean bricks so it will be above the pond

This 3-foot waterfall flanked by ferns is powered by a pump that recirculates almost 300 gallons of water an hour, the capacity of a 5-by-8-foot pond. The waterfall was designed by Gordon Ledbetter. (Photo by Charles B. Thomas)

floor, where debris settles. Then just plug the electrical cord into an outlet, and the pump will begin recirculating water. The manufacturer lists the amps required to *operate* the pump, but starting up the system requires substantially more power; the electrical circuit must have reserve capacity beyond what is needed for operation, especially if the pump uses more than 8 amps. Residential circuits are usually 15 amps. If the circuit is overloaded, the breaker will turn off the current. The power source for the pump should be at least 6 feet from the edge of the pond; the electrical cord should be at least 10 feet long. It can be plugged into any standard three-prong household electrical outlet, but *for your safety the outlet must have a ground-fault circuit interrupter* (installed by a licensed electrician), which will shut off the circuit if it senses that water has come in contact with any of the wiring.

In winter in the frost belt, the earth warms the water on the bottom of the pond, and fish seek warmth there. (In the summer the earth cools the water at the bottom.) If you leave the pump on in the winter, the circulation will cool the bottom water, and the fish, especially koi, may suffer. In the frost belt you should disconnect the pump, clean it, and store it indoors until spring.

Calculating Pump Power and Lift

Here are factors to take into account when deciding on the size of the pump your pond requires.

The pump fittings must be compatible (possibly by using an adapter) with the filter you have chosen, and the pump must be powerful enough to move all the pond water through the filter within two hours for a mechanical filter or within four to six hours for a biological filter.

The pump needs to have enough power to move the water through the piping or tubing to the filter, and in some cases, beyond the filter to the highest and farthest points you want to reach above or outside the pond. Each 10 feet of horizontal distance takes as much power as 1 foot of vertical lift, as given in the table.

Pump Power and Lift

Horsepower	Watts	Amps	GPH lifted				
			1 ft.	3 ft.	5 ft.	10 ft.	15 ft.
1/125	36	0.6	170	140	100	—	—
1/40	100	1.7	300	255	205	70	—
1/37	20[a]	0.4[a]	288	214	117	—	—
1/15	220	3.3	500	435	337	210	65
1/11	68[a]	0.7[a]	730	634	540	380	—
1/6	380	5.0	1,200	1,170	1,100	1,000	840
3/10	720	9.0[b]	3,000	—	2,750	1,750	750
2/5	830	10.0[c]	3,400	—	3,250	2,500	1,550
1/2	1,100	11.0[d]	—	—	4,200	3,800	2,700

a. Super-energy-efficient models having ceramic parts and no oil.
b. Needs 13 amps to start. (Residential circuits are usually 15 amps.)
c. Needs 14 amps to start.
d. Needs 40 amps to start.

The pump needs sufficient power to move the water through the statuary or fountain or up to the waterfall or watercourse you have chosen to return the water to the pond. Suppliers of fountainheads and piped statuary will tell you how many gallons per hour (GPH) are needed for proper functioning of a particular piece.

If you are returning the water over a waterfall or through a watercourse, plan on having enough pumping capacity to maintain a certain depth to the flow of water. Recirculating 300 gallons an hour will create a ½-inch-deep flow of water over a ledge 3 inches wide; over a ledge 6 inches wide, the water will be ¼ inch deep; over a ledge 1 foot wide, there will be only a trickle of water. By doubling the capacity, using a pump rated at 600 gallons per hour, you can have a ½-inch flow — deep enough to be attractive — over a 6-inch-wide waterfall or a ¼-inch flow over a 12-inch-wide ledge.

Every filter needs a compatible pump, and every pump has a specific capacity to move water expressed in gallons per hour. The higher a pump must lift the water, the slower it operates, as the table below demonstrates.

Manufacturers' specifications differ, so study them to make sure the pump you choose meets all your needs. The table shows the amps and watts needed to operate various pond pumps, and the capacity of typical models to lift and move water. The first line of the table tells you that a particular recirculating pump with $\frac{1}{125}$ horsepower that operates on 36 watts of electricity can be expected to lift about 170 gallons of water 1 foot high in an hour or 140 gallons 3 feet high in an hour or 100 gallons 5 feet high in an hour. Remember, each 10 feet the water must travel horizontally has the same effect on capacity in gallons per hour as lifting water 1 foot vertically.

The Sounds of Water

A waterfall is a popular way to help screen a filter from view and to bring the sounds and sparkle of water into the garden. You'll see more birds if you have a waterfall; they love the sound of the water, and the shallows at the edge of the falls provide a drinking place.

The falls needn't be high to be effective — 1 to 3 feet is typical. The most appealing waterfall is in scale with its pond, and trickles or tumbles from a rustic mound that nature appears to have covered with velvety mosses, ferns, and other moisture-loving plants. The lower pond should be larger than any higher pond. An obviously contrived waterfall makes you

An ornate metal bubbler fed by a small pump quietly aerates the water it returns to a shallow pond. The black pump is almost invisible against the pond's black liner. (Photo by Alex Lewis)

wish it weren't there. Water lilies love still water and resent endless waves, so keep the return of the water to the pond gentle or allow some distance between the water's turbulent reentry point and the lilies. Or, place a smooth stone barrier between the waves made by the reentry of the water and the water lilies.

Arrange the waterfall so that you have easy access to the filter. Use rigid PVC pipe to conduct the water to the top of the waterfall. To return the water to the pond, place a liner of rubber or PVC, the flexible kind, underneath the waterfall or watercourse. All the water must be returned to the pond — don't let any escape. Cover the waterfall liner with local stones, if available, but don't use limestone, for it will raise the pH of the water. The sound of the waterfall will be enhanced if it juts out over the pond a bit. This creates a sound chamber behind the spot where the falling water hits the surface.

Sun dancing on a jet of spray and the water music of bubblers and water-spilling statuary have their own particular charms. Bubblers are delightful in tubs and small containers, and a spray head that tosses water a few feet into the air looks great in almost any garden pond. There are two- and three-tier sprays, and sprays that sheet the water out in the form of a bell or a shell. Water moving through a metal or stone form — fish, frog, or water lily — and gently spilling or energetically gurgling back into the pond can be very attractive in a well-landscaped garden. Use rigid PVC piping if the water is to be moved outside of the pond perimeter and buried out of sight; flexible tubing will collapse if rocks are placed over it or if it is walked on.

Water at Night

Lighted at night, a water garden takes on the mystery and romance of moonlight. The magic is achieved by simple low-voltage underwater lighting equipment with a transformer that runs on the same electrical outlet that powers your pump. The easiest installation is a light equipped with a timer that turns the lights on and off automatically. Choose noncorrodible equipment on a sturdy base and use the installation only in conjunction with a ground-fault circuit interrupter.

The most romantic night lights are underwater units with one to three outlets for 36-watt bulbs that quietly glow up

The classical statue, the symmetrical plantings, matching fountains, and moongate entrance lend an air of formality to the garden. Among the marginal plants used are pickerel rush and cattails. (Photo by Bill Heritage)

A powerful pump sustains this classic fountain. This much turbulence would be too much for water lilies but will not disturb marginal plants. (Photo by Elvin McDonald)

through the water, just bright enough to outline the floating lilies on the surface and a few of the marginal plants. Use light bulbs that have a life expectancy of 4,000 hours or more; lower-rated bulbs must be replaced too often.

Another option is to place a hanging lantern or a covered light on a post in a position where the light is reflected by the splashing of a fountain or a waterfall. Like moonlight, the light will make a path across the water.

Insurance Against Ice

In Zones 3 through 7 there may be the danger of ice covering the pond for more than three or four consecutive days. A little ice isn't bad, but if it covers the surface completely, the pond cannot breathe. Like lungs, the surface of the pond disperses carbon dioxide wastes from the creatures that live underwater and gases released by organic decay, and it absorbs from the atmosphere the oxygen that the creatures need. When ice covers the surface, the exchange cannot take place.

To assure air for the fish, use a de-icer that will keep some of the pond surface ice-free at all times. A de-icer is a simple heating element attached to a flotation device. The best de-icers are equipped with thermostats so that they turn on only when warmth is needed. The most popular are rated at 1,500 watts. Float the de-icer only during the weeks or months when warmth is needed, and always use a ground-fault circuit interrupter with it.

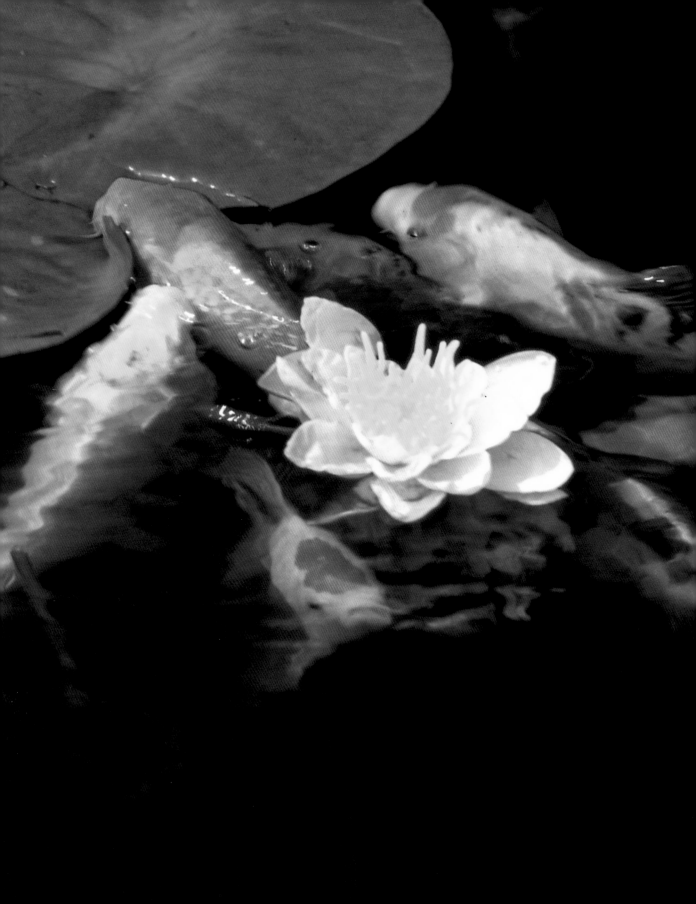

5 🌀 Planting, Stocking, and Maintaining the Garden

WATER GARDENING is especially inviting to new gardeners because it is so easy to learn what you need to know to have a truly lovely pond. The number of popular outstanding ornamental aquatic plants in North America doesn't go much beyond the two hundred or so described in the chapters in Part II. And the general information on planting, culture, winter care, and maintenance that follows applies to just about all of them.

Once the pond is filled, with filter and pump in place if you are using them and the water returning musically to the pond via a waterfall, statuary, bubbler, or other means, it's time to plant and stock the garden. If you are ordering from a mail order supplier, the company will hold living stock until you are ready for the plants and then for the fish and other creatures. If you are buying from a local aquatic nursery, you should check with them ahead of time to find out whether they will have the plants and fish you want when you are ready for them. The magic formula below lists the proportions of each

These gorgeous koi are greedy and aggressive when it comes to food. Having lots of submerged plants and relatively few fish is the best way to promote clear water. (Photo by Susan Elder)

element that will bring the water garden into balance in four to eight weeks. (Odd as it seems, aquatic nurseries and pet shops sell fish by the inch!)

The Magic Formula

For every 1 to 2 square feet of pond surface, you'll need:

> 1 bunch (6 stems each) of submerged plants
>
> 1 black Japanese snail
>
> 2 inches of fish for fish *up to 6 inches long*
>
> $\frac{1}{10}$ of a small or medium-size water lily (1 lily per 10–20 square feet)
>
> $\frac{1}{3}$ of a marginal or a small floating-leaved plant (1 plant for every 3–6 square feet)

According to the formula, a typical garden pond, one that has about 100 square feet of surface (10 by 10 feet), would have the following quantities:

> 50–100 bunches of submerged plants
>
> 50–100 black Japanese snails
>
> 100–200 inches of fish in assorted sizes *up to 6 inches long*
>
> 5–10 water lilies
>
> 18–33 marginal and/or floating-leaved plants (perhaps 3 each of the varieties chosen)

Use the formula with a liberal dose of common sense. For submerged plants and snails, the numbers are the essential minimum. You may want to add the other small creatures described in Chapter 10. They are sold in aquatic nurseries and pet shops. The figures for fish are maximums. For the ornamentals — the floating-leaved plants and the upright marginals — the recommended amounts may be increased or reduced by 50 percent, according to how much open water and foliage you want to see. Smaller ponds are generally stocked more heavily than larger ponds; a single small lily will cover 90 percent of the surface of a 2-foot-square tub. The larger the pond, the more open water you can have without sacrificing plant variety. A pond that has 100 square feet of surface may have about 60 to 70 percent floating cover. But in a 20-by-50-foot pond — 1,000 square feet of surface — you can afford the luxury of having half the water not covered.

When you have calculated your order for fish, cross-check the quantities using these figures: for every inch of goldfish there should be at least 3 to 5 gallons of water. For every inch of koi or golden orfe, the pond should have at least 6 to 10 gallons of water. These figures assume that the fish will be of assorted sizes, *but not longer than 6 inches.* For larger fish, you need more gallons per inch: each additional inch of big fish places more demands on the pond environment than each inch of smaller fish; each additional 10 percent in length might make a 30 percent greater demand on the pond. Six to eight goldfish, five or six golden orfe, and two or three koi is a good mix for the average 10-by-10-foot pond. For a tub garden, two or three goldfish 2 to 3 inches long are enough.

The more fish you have, the more likely it is that the water will be greener than you want it to be. By increasing the number of plants, especially submerged plants, you will have fewer green-water woes. *The key to clear water is to have plenty of submerged plants and relatively few fish.*

Planting the Pond

Place the plants in the water garden as soon as the pond is filled so that the various processes that ready the pond to receive fish and snails can begin. The chlorine products used to treat drinking water are safe for plants but not for fish, as explained in Chapter 3.

The Containers

Aquatics are planted in soil in shallow pans, deeper pails, and large tubs. (Container sizes are measured in quarts.) These are placed in the pond at the depths recommended in the plant chapters. The containers do not need holes for drainage or water circulation, but one or two nail holes should be made in containers for marginal plants if these are placed on a shelf where the water level may drop below the rim of the container. The hole in the bottom of the container assures the plant of adequate water.

The table will help you choose containers for your plantings and help you decide how many plants of each type to put into each container. The general rule is the larger the container (especially at the top), the longer you can wait to divide plants. Plants also may be set out in used well-scrubbed garden pots — clay or plastic — if you block the drainage holes with stones. There's no need to seal them. Containers for submerged plants and other small aquatics should be at least 4 inches deep. Plant only one variety in each container, for most aquatic plants are aggressive spreaders, and one kind is bound to crowd out the other types.

Soil and Fertilizing

The best planting medium for soil-rooted aquatics is heavy garden soil that is free of peat, manures, vermiculite, or any material that might float. Use sand for planting submerged plants. Avoid commercial potting mixes. Most ornamental aquatics are tolerant of soils with a pH range of 6.0 to 8.0. Research by the staff at Lilypons Water Gardens has shown that the optimum pH of soil and pond water is 6.5 to 7.5. This range is suitable for a wide selection of aquatic plant and animal life. If the pH of your pond is over 7.5, continue to

Containers for Aquatic Plants

Container	Size	No. of submerged plants	No. of water lilies	No. of floating-leaved plants or upright marginals (or lotus)
3.5-qt. pan	8″ diam. 5.5″ deep	6	None	1 to 2
7.5-qt. pan	10″ diam. 7″ deep	9–12	1 small	2 to 3
9-qt. pan	10.5″ diam. 8.75″ deep	12	1 small or medium	3
17.5-qt. pan	12.6″ diam. 9.1″ deep	16	1 any size	3 to 4 (or 1 small lotus)
10-qt. pan	13″ wide 15″ long 5″ deep	12	1 small or medium	3 to 4
14-qt. pan	13″ wide 15″ long 6.5″ deep	18	1 small plus 1 medium, or 1 large	3 to 4 (or 1 small lotus)
19-qt. pan	16.25″ diam. 7″ deep	20	1 or 2 any size	3 to 5 (or 1 large or small lotus)
48-qt. pan	23″ diam. 7″ deep	48	1 to 3 any size	6 to 12 (or 1 large or small lotus)
5-qt. pail	9″ diam. 6″ deep	6	1 small	1
11-qt. pail	11″ diam. 9″ deep	9	1 small or medium	3
22-qt. tub	16.5″ diam. 9.25″ deep	24	2 small or 1 medium, or 1 large	3 to 5 floating or 6–10 upright (or 1 large or small lotus)
30-qt. tub	19″ diam. 9″ deep	30	2 small or 1 medium, or 1 large	3 to 5 floating or 6–10 upright (or 1 large or small lotus)

monitor it; if it rises above 8, you should treat it, as explained in Chapter 3. Fertilizer for aquatics comes in tablet form in nitrogen-phosphate-potash formulations (NPK) of 10-14-8. When you plant, push tablets into the soil of each container as directed on the fertilizer label.

When you plant the containers, work in a shady place near your pond. Be sure not to damage the growing tips of plants such as water lilies, lotus, and irises, and leave the tips just above the soil line. Cover the soil with ½ inch of *rinsed* gravel that is ½ to ¾ inch in diameter. (Place gravel in a colander and rinse it with a hose.) Using water from the pond, soak the soil-filled container thoroughly to dislodge air pockets before placing it in the pond; this will also help to avoid clouding the water. You'll know the air pockets have been displaced when the bubbling stops.

More specific instructions for planting the ornamentals are given in Part Two.

Into the Pond

Plan the placement of the plants before you place the containers in the pond. The water lily containers should be several feet apart, depending on the ultimate size of the plants and how much open water you want. The upright marginal plants need only a foot or two between them on the pond floor or shelf: generally they are grouped to one side and toward the back of the pond, away from the house. Each container should be raised to the height that will place the growing tips of the plants at the required water depth. You can use smooth, large stones, clean bricks, or weathered cinderblocks (new ones will raise the water pH) to make platforms on the pond floor. If you have built a shelf into the pond, set the containers on it, adding platforms as needed when you run out of shelf space.

The soaked containers will be far heavier than most land plants, so have someone help you move them into the pond. It's a good idea to wear old sneakers or rubber boots for working in the pond. Once the containers are in the water, slide or float them to their locations.

Allow the plants a few weeks in the pond to develop, then decide how you like your composition. From a design point of view, planting a water garden is a little like decorating a room: you have a mental picture of how the furniture should look, but it usually needs some shifting before the room is completely satisfying. Repositioning plants in the water garden is as simple as moving furniture and a lot easier on your back. Don't lift the containers out of the water; it's much easier to move them suspended in the water a few inches above the floor of the pond.

The Submerged Plants

The submerged plants are the first aquatics to be placed in the new pond. Except for *Vallisneria* and dwarf sagittaria, which are sold individually, submerged plants come in bunches of six stems secured by a rubber band. Each stem with foliage is about 6 inches high, and from ¼ inch to 1 inch across. If you can't place them in the pond right away, they'll keep for about two weeks in a container of water in a cool area out of the direct sun.

Use the table on page 69 as a guide to the number of containers you will need. If you are planting in old pans or pails of your own, allow about 6 square inches of container surface for every bunch of submerged plants. To protect your submerged plants from being nibbled to death by big koi and goldfish, use plastic mesh sold by aquatic plant suppliers to create domed containers. The plants will grow through the mesh; this will allow the fish to graze without eating all the foliage.

The best planting medium for submerged plants, which feed not through roots but through their leaves, is clean sand. The roots serve primarily as anchors, and in cooler regions they provide nourishment for the plants through the winter. Working in a shady place, rinse the bundles of submerged plants gently with a hose, and remove the rubber band. Gently press each bunch or stem about 2 inches into the sand. *Do not add fertilizer.* Fill each container with sand to within an inch or so of its rim, and top the sand with *rinsed* gravel. Add pond water to the container to displace trapped air.

Gently lower the planted containers to the pond floor and distribute them fairly evenly, avoiding areas that you later plan to have shaded with floating-leaved plants. Submerged plants need sun, and you should be able to easily see the plants from above. Placing them so that there is 1 to 2 feet of water over the gravel is usually best. If the strands elongate and become puny, raise the containers to where they receive more direct sunlight.

When the submerged plants purchased as bunched cuttings are 8 inches or taller and growing well, you can take 5- or 6-inch cuttings and multiply your assets. At any time during the growing season you can break off the top 5 or 6 inches of a plant, press the ends into containers filled with sand, and repeat the planting process.

The five submerged plants recommended below are among the best for starving out greenwater algae. They are also quite lovely; think of them as ornamental foliage rather like ferns and astilbes. You could plant just one kind, but the diversity of these five adds interest to the water garden and makes it more attractive. Use a separate container for each variety. With the exception of the little sagittaria, these all grow stems 2 to 3 feet long.

Be cautious in putting other algae-clearing plants into your pond. Those that compete well with the algae absorb a lot of nutrients and may be invasive. Regrettably for water gardeners, two of the most beautiful algae clearers — water hyacinth and water lettuce (discussed in Chapter 7) — are illegal in some states. If they are legal where you live, add them to the list that follows. Federal statute forbids the shipment of water hyacinth in interstate commerce.

Cabomba caroliniana
Washington grass
ZONES 6–11

This pretty aquatic foliage plant has deeply divided lacy leaves that grow in a fan shape. It bears tiny white or, in some forms, purple flowers. The foliage is a favorite spawning place and banquet table for fish, so provide a mesh dome if you have goldfish or koi over 6 inches long. *Cabomba* grows wild in ponds and slow streams from Michigan to Texas, Florida, and the Carolinas. It can become a pest, so don't plant it in the wild anywhere. This is good advice for all the submerged plants mentioned in this book.

Cabomba caroliniana,
Washington grass.

Elodea canadensis var. *gigantea*
Anacharis
ZONES 5–11

Sometimes referred to by an earlier botanical name, *Anacharis canadensis,* this graceful plant has slim, fernlike fronds covered with dark green leaves. It is such a good filter that it eventually

Elodea canadensis *var.* gigantea, *anacharis.*

Myriophyllum *species.*

may appear brownish. A gentle hosing or shaking will restore the color. Elodea grows right up to the top of the water and blooms at the tips of thin stems. Each three-petaled white flower is half the diameter of a shirt button and has a yellow dot in the middle. Its foliage is another favorite fish food, so protect the containers with plastic domes. Found from Quebec southward through most of temperate North America, it is a good submerged plant for both cooler regions and the deep South.

Myriophyllum species
Water milfoil

Zones 4–11, depending on species

Several species are planted in water gardens for their graceful foliage, their efficiency in filtering out debris, and their appetite for pond nutrients. Now and then the delicate, hairlike leaves that cover the stems may need to be gently hosed until clean. Fish love to swim through *Myriophyllum* and to lay eggs there. They're also known to eat the plants, so provide protective domes. *Myriophyllum aquatica,* parrot's-feather, is not considered a submerged plant because nearly all of its foliage rests above the water surface. It is described in Chapter 7.

Sagittaria subulata
Dwarf sagittaria

Zones 5–11

Dwarf sagittaria belongs to a group of shallow-water plants that bear quite lovely flowers. This energetic species, just 3 to 6 inches tall, thrives at the water's edge and underwater as well. In marshy land it spreads so rapidly that it is used as a soil stabilizer.

Vallisneria americana,
wild celery.

Vallisneria americana
Wild celery
ZONES 4–11

Vallisneria is a beautiful plant whose ribbonlike leaves are excellent filters and sway with the movement of the water, stirred by passing fish. It is sold as an individual plant, not as a cutting, and by means of stolons spreads to form a pleasant green carpet. The species grows freely in quiet water from New Brunswick to North Dakota, and south to the Gulf states.

The Ornamental Plants
The outstanding ornamental plants grown in North American water gardens are presented in Chapters 6 through 11. The order of those chapters reflects the order in which you might choose your plants. The plants that float their foliage and flowers over the surface of the pond — the lilies, the small floating-leaved plants, and the lotus — are presented in Chapters 6, 7, and 8. All together, these plants should cover a third to a half of the surface of a large pond and two-thirds of the surface of a smaller pond.

The irises and other marginal plants in Chapter 9 are upright aquatics used as linear accents to edge and backdrop the water garden. Like land plants, they're chosen for texture as well as form and for the movement they bring to the pond's vertical plane. Some, such as the irises and equisetum, are narrow-leaved, while others, like the huge elephant's-ear, have broad leaves. Although the magic formula suggests a numerical range for these plants, the right number for your pond is a matter of personal taste. Start with fewer than you think you will want. Most aquatic plants are fast-growing. Remember, the display will be far more satisfying if you plant three of one type in each container rather than one. The verticals especially look lonely and sometimes spindly when planted singly. If you mix different types in a single container, you risk having the most aggressive grower crowd out the others.

Some aquatic plants are sold already planted and growing in pans or pails, but most come as bareroot plants packed in moist materials in a plastic bag. Mail order houses will ship them at about the right time for planting in your climate. Spring is the best time to plant most aquatics and see them bloom the first season. But if you are creating your pond in summer, you can plant it up to a month before the first frost. The hardy plants can go into the pond in spring as soon as the water becomes warm enough to work in comfortably, about 55 degrees. Annuals and tender perennials such as the tropical water lilies are planted after the pond water is holding steady above 69 degrees or at the temperatures recommended in Part Two for that plant.

Releasing Fish and Other Small Helpers

After the plants are in the pond but before you add the fish, snails, and frogs, let the water age for a week or two to allow helpful bacteria to colonize the pond walls. Or to save time you can add bottled bacteria, which is available from aquatic plant dealers.

Before you add fish or other aquatic animals to the pond, as a preventive measure it's a good idea to put into the water a broad-spectrum fish disease remedy. Thereafter you should not add remedies unless the fish seem listless or have red spots or a white fungus growth. Pet shops and aquatic nurseries sell well-established remedies for such ills, but in a properly stocked pond they're not common.

Most large pet shops sell hardy fish that survive year round in water gardens. Aquatic nurseries and mail order specialists sell fish, tadpoles, and scavengers as well. The best seasons for shipping fish are spring and fall. When they arrive, float the bag in which they have traveled on the pond for about fifteen minutes to allow the fish to adjust gradually to the pond temperature. Gently cover the bag with a newspaper or towel to prevent solar heat from building up inside. However, if the water in the bag is cloudy and the fish are obviously in distress and gasping for air at the surface, release them into the pond immediately. For the first ten days, feed the fish lightly with an antibiotic-treated food.

Snails are shipped only when there is no danger that they will freeze or overheat, generally when the water temperature is between 40 and 80 degrees. Snails are not nearly as sensitive to temperature changes as are goldfish, orfe, and koi. However, you should take the same care in releasing them into the pond as you would for fish. They are shipped in bags with a little water or in moist packing materials and will seem dormant when unpacked. If they arrive in a bag with water, follow the procedure described above for fish. If they are shipped in a packing material, rinse them in pond water and gently slip them into the pond. Live snails will sink to the bottom; any that are dead will float up and should be removed. It may take the snails about three days to recover from traveling and go into action.

Where the pond surface freezes solid for more than three or four days in a row, use a de-icer to keep some part of the pond open. You can leave the fish, snails, tadpoles and frogs to their long winter nap, or you can move the fish indoors to a large fish tank equipped with an aerator. Place a screen over the tank to prevent the fish from jumping out of their winter home.

Maintenance: The Pond Year
Spring

In the frost belt the first spring chore is to get the mechanical and electrical equipment — filter, pump, air pump, and night lights — out of storage and return them to the pond.

Add water to the pond if the level is lower than normal. Before adding tap water to the pond, remember to add a neutralizing agent for the chlorine, chloramine, or chlorine dioxide used in the water supply. If the water is treated with chlorine and if the fish have been kept indoors for the winter, you can add plain tap water and let it sit for several days before reintroducing the fish.

Spring is the time to lift and groom your water garden plants. The perennials should be divided every two or three years in Zones 3 to 8, but in Zones 9 to 11, where growth can be phenomenal, they will need to be divided annually. If you have planted in large tubs instead of the smaller pans, you can wait twice as long before dividing the plants. Fertilize the plants and return them to their usual places in the water.

The fish will become active when the water temperature rises above 44 degrees. When you see that they are active, you may resume feeding them.

Spring/Summer

Clear the filter regularly — daily, weekly, or bimonthly, according to the type of filter and the demands of the pond.

Fertilize the plants twice a month for lotus and once a month for the lilies (but once a week for *Victorias*) and most others; do not fertilize the submerged plants. When the water temperature is over 75 degrees, fertilize the lilies and the lotus twice a month.

Pinch off yellowing leaves and dead flowers as they occur, leaving nothing to decay in the water. In water lilies, new young leaves continuously sprout from the flowering center, then stretch out as new leaves rise. As the leaves fade in color, they are no longer doing their job and should be removed. When left in the pond, they decay and become food for undesirable algae. Speedy removal of dead flowers seems to encourage flowering.

Fall

If there is an inch or more of debris on the bottom of your pond, empty and clean it while the weather is still warm enough to make the work pleasant. Disconnect the filter and use the pump and its tubing to empty the water downhill. Remember to be mindful of your neighbors, who may not want your pond water. The nutrients in the water are beneficial to garden plants, so spill it where it will do the most good. When the water is down to the last few inches, net the fish, snails, and other creatures and place them in a large open container filled with pond water. Cover it with netting to prevent the fish from jumping out of their temporary quarters; use an aerator to provide them with oxygen.

You may want to enlist some energetic friends to help you lift the plants. Cover them with moist newspaper after removing discolored foliage, spent flowers, and stems.

After clearing the silt and leaves from the bottom, refill the pond, adding a dechlorinating agent. Gradually blend some of this water into the container holding the fish. When the water temperature is the same as that of the pond, the fish can safely be returned.

If you are in a frost-free area, groom and fertilize the plants before returning them to the pond for an active winter season.

In the frost belt, when the late-blooming tropical lilies are killed by repeated frosts, discard them and other tender perennials. Chapter 6 has information on continuing the tropicals from year to year. Cut back the hardy plants soon after frosts spoil them and lower the containers to a depth that will not freeze. If the pond isn't deep enough for that, move the plants in their containers to a cool, frost-free garage or basement on a day when the air temperature is in the forties. Cover the plants with damp cloths or newspapers and enclose the containers in plastic trash bags. Check them periodically during the winter to make sure the plants aren't drying out. Return them to the pond in spring when the the goldfish begin eating regularly — when the afternoon water temperature is above 45 degrees.

Winter

If ice threatens, you can cover the pond until the coldest weather is past if you wish. Place 2-by-4 boards across the pond to support a tarp or canvas or other material. Leaves placed on top and held in place with netting will act as insulation. Secure the arrangement so it can withstand winter winds. Mark the pond covering well so guests don't accidentally walk over it. Be sure to allow a ventilation space on the side of the pond away from the prevailing wind direction. *Don't* seal the pond off completely. Gases in the water must have an escape route, and fresh air must be available for the fish.

In frost-free regions you should keep the pump and filter in place and working through the winter. If you have a biological filter, give it a thorough cleaning at the coolest point during the winter.

Part Two

The Aquatic Plants and Pond Creatures

6 🐚 Nymphaea: The Water Lilies

In the lily pond at Longwood Gardens, the bright green pads of the hardy lilies and the streaked foliage of the tropicals are dwarfed by the huge floating leaves of Victoria. In the background is a spectacular stand of upright lotus leaves and flowers. (Photo courtesy of L. Albee, Longwood Gardens)

Some flowers have an evocative quality that entangles the mind and captures the senses. The classical proportions of a starlike white water lily floating on or just above the still waters of a pond imparts a sense of serenity and purity. Lilies are the celebrities of the water garden. From spring until fall when the pond water temperature is in the mid-60s or warmer, lily buds rise one by one to the surface and unfold their petals with stately grace. The third or fourth day after opening, the blossom remains closed, slowly sinks, and never opens again. Many water lily varieties have a sweet haunting fragrance.

The common names that have come down to us through the centuries are water lily and, from ancient Greek mythology, water-nymph. *Nymphaea* is the botanical name of the genus, but the hundreds of hybrids floating on our ponds are sold under their cultivar names. A cultivar, or cultivated variety, is designated by single quotes around the name, for example, 'Virginia'. Not too many years ago, you could count on the fingers of one hand the new water lily hybrids introduced each year. The soaring popularity of water gardens has encouraged hybridizing, and now dozens of glorious new lilies are presented every spring. The great names associated with hybridizing are Latour Marliac and George H. Pring, the first two people inducted into the International Water Lily Hall of Fame.

Latour Marliac was the most outstanding hybridizer of hardy lilies in *Nymphaea* history. Working in the late 1800s and early 1900s in Temple-sur-Lot, a small town near Bordeaux in southwestern France, Marliac produced many of the hybrids that are popular today. His multipetaled 'Gloire de Temple-sur-Lot' is one of the most beautiful lilies we know. George Pring was superintendent of the Missouri Botanic Garden in St. Louis for many years. Orchids were his first interest, but to maintain the humidity in the botanic garden's glass house he put in water lilies — and fell in love with them. His name is associated especially with tropical water lilies.

The names encountered most often in the literature of the beautiful modern hybrids are those of Perry Slocum and Dr. Kirk Strawn. Slocum, a medical student at Cornell University in the 1930s, became so interested in the aquatic plants on his father's farm that he gave up medicine and founded the famous Slocum Water Gardens in New York State. After productive years in Florida, he now is hybridizing lotus and water lilies in North Carolina. Strawn, a Texan, is a prolific hybridizer of hardy water lilies. Two California hybridizers are responsible for many of today's magnificent tropical lily introductions: Martin E. Randig, who worked in the San Bernardino Valley in the middle of this century, and Jack Wood, who in 1988 retired as owner of a California aquatic nursery.

Water lily blossoms range in size from as small as a pansy to twice as large as your hand. There are star shapes and

Historic 'Gloire de Temple-sur-Lot'. (Photo by Michael Elspas)

cup shapes, blossoms as fluffy as a powder puff or as spiky as a cactus flower. The historic 'Gloire de Temple-sur-Lot' has one hundred petals. All water lilies have a center of gilded stamens that stand up straight when the flower is new, then slowly fold inward as they age. The position of the stamens tells you the age of the flower.

There are two distinct groups of water lilies: the hardy ones, which are frost-tolerant perennials, and the tropicals, which are frost-tender perennials. To bloom well, tropical lilies need three or more weeks of temperatures above 80 degrees. The hardy lilies and the tropicals are similar but not related closely enough to cross-breed naturally. Each has a specific role and its own particular virtues in the water garden. Both need sun to produce flowers, but a few hardy lilies will bloom with as little as three or four hours of sun a day. In spells of cool, cloudy weather, flowering may be a little slow, but this often is followed by a period of profuse blooming.

The hardy water lilies are open only during the day, while the tropical lilies may be either day- or night-flowering plants. The hardy lilies and the day-blooming tropicals open around nine in the morning and close between three and five in the afternoon. The night-blooming tropicals are favorites with people who are home mostly in the evening. They unfold as the stars come out and stay open until late morning or early afternoon. In frost-free areas, both hardy and tropical water lilies bloom year-round, year after year, though less generously during the cold months.

In the frost belt the hardy water lilies return every spring. They are usually the first plants chosen for the water garden and are accorded the best places. Though tropical water lilies die where there is repeated frost and must be replaced every year, they are desirable because they outbloom hardy lilies. The largest and most fragrant flowers are found among the tropicals — immense platters sometimes reaching 12 inches in diameter. And the tropicals will provide an extra month or two of bloom after the hardies have fallen asleep in the fall. Tropicals love hot weather, but once established where the water cools gradually at the end of the season — even in Minnesota or New England — they become hardened and will go on blooming in water well below 70 degrees.

For a new pond's first summer, plant only lilies that are gorgeous, easy, and sure to flower. If there's space for six lilies and you have budget constraints, begin with two hardy lilies and one tropical. The pond needn't start with a full complement. Try the hardy 'Pink Beauty', an exquisite shell-pink lily that blooms freely even the first season. The most loved of all the hardy lilies, 'Pink Beauty' adapts easily to ponds large and small. 'Dauben', a lovely soft blue-violet tropical, is another virtually infallible bloomer. With as little as three to four hours of direct sunlight a day, it will probably produce more blossoms than a hardy lily in your pond's first season. The combination of 'Pink Beauty' and 'Dauben' is exquisite.

For the pond's second season add two more tropical lilies and another hardy. Any of the blue tropical lilies and a white will complement the colors of the hardy lilies. You are sure to enjoy the tropical night-blooming 'Wood's White Knight', whose profuse, exceptionally beautiful large white flowers with soft, yellow stamens seem luminous on the dark water. The second or third year the hardy lilies will produce many more blooms. But you may want to pinch them back to recover open water so you can install more lilies or a lotus you've just discovered you can't live without.

Shading the Pond

We plant water lilies and other plants with floating foliage and flowers for our pleasure, but they also shade the pond and absorb nutrients. These services help curb green water and therefore contribute to the balance of the ecosystem. Open water enhances the beauty of the pond, and the rule is, the larger the pond, the more open water it can have: 60 to 70 percent *total* floating cover is recommended for a pond that is about 10 by 10 feet; about 50 percent *total* floating cover is enough for a pond about 20 by 50 feet.

If you see lily pads and hardy blossoms standing 2 to 3 inches above the surface of the pond, you'll know that the plants have become overcrowded and the rootstock needs to be divided. The blossoms of some hardy lilies like 'Virginia' and 'Charlene Strawn' typically stand 1 to 2 inches above the water. But when their pads also are held high, even though the rhizomes are 12 or more inches under water, that's a sign that the plants need dividing.

Cutting Flowers

Water lilies last longest as cut flowers if they are picked the first day they open, when the stamens are erect — and if you play a trick on them. Plunge your arm straight down and pinch off one of the semirubbery stems about a foot long. Holding the flower upright by the stem in one hand and a lighted candle in the other, let a drop of hot wax fall on the base of the blossom between each petal. When the flower's closing time comes in late afternoon, the hardened wax wedge will keep the petals open. Place the stems of hardy lilies in water to within 1 inch of the base of the flower; the tropicals should have water to within 3 inches of the base. Out of sun and drafts, water lilies usually stay fresh for three or four days. If there is fragrance, it is most noticeable the first day.

The Best Hardy Water Lilies

The hardy water lilies are the first to send their sinuous green-to-brown stalks to the pond surface to unfold lily pads in spring. They come into bloom when the pond water temperatures are steadily in the sixties and above. In Zone 8 the hardy lilies begin to flower in April and continue until early Novem-

'Chromatella', like most hardy water lilies, floats on the water, while the tropical lily 'Red Flare' holds its blooms well above the surface.

ber. In Zone 6 they come into flower around mid-May and stop in September. In colder zones the season is shortened at both ends. In frost-free zones they bloom at a slower rate during winter.

The most romantic water lilies are the virginal whites, but there are gorgeous lilies in shades and variations on themes of yellow, apricot, pink, and red. A fascinating small group of yellow to red hardy lilies are known as changeables. The first morning the changeables open yellow or bronze, then melt to sunset colors and deeper reds on the second and third day of blooming. All water lilies except the white ones modify their coloring from day to day, some getting darker, some lighter, but only those that shift color from yellow to red are classed as changeables. The juvenile leaves of some lilies are handsomely mottled or flecked, and many of these change as they age until they are all green.

The water lilies recommended here are those that best resist pests and diseases. They have been chosen for their prolific flowering, lasting bloom period, and magnificent colors. Over the last several years, the most consistently popular hardy lilies have been the pink 'Hollandia' and 'Pink Beauty'; the white 'Virginia' and 'Virginalis'; the yellow 'Charlene Strawn' and 'Chrometella'; the red 'James Brydon' and 'Attraction', and the changeable 'Comanche'.

The hardy water lilies described below are beautiful and relatively carefree in Zones 4 to 11. Some lilies grow naturally in Zone 3 and probably could survive in a pond 3 to 5 feet deep, but they won't winter over successfully in a water garden 15 to 30 inches deep. In Zone 3 they are taken in for the winter, as described on page 116. A few water lilies can't stand really hot weather.

Exotic changeables: 'Sioux', below, in its early colors, and 'Paul Hariot', right, after the color has changed to russet.

The water lilies are grouped by size, meaning the square feet of pond surface they will cover when fully developed in a typical home water garden. The area a lily will cover is influenced by the amount of surface area allowed, fertilizer, water temperature and stillness, the size of the container in which the rhizome is planted, and the amount of sunlight.

Pygmy (less than 3 square feet)

Water lilies in this size category must struggle to cover the surface of a barrel water garden. They are ideal plants for the small, wonderful world of the tub garden. In a 20-acre lake, a pygmy will occupy 2 to 3 square feet, and the blooms will still be the size of a half dollar and the leaves about 3 to 4 inches across. Pygmy species don't multiply easily, so few nurseries offer them. If you want a very small lily but can't find one, plant any of the small or small-medium types that dwarf themselves when growing in a restricted space.

White

Nymphaea tetragona
ZONES 4–11

This true pygmy bears exquisite little star-shaped, single white flowers 1½ to 2½ inches across. The lily pads, no wider than 3 to 4 inches, are yellow on the underside. Though it is native to Maine, Alaska, Ontario, Siberia, and Japan, *N. tetragona* is difficult to grow in most of the United States. It survives cold winters but doesn't like hot weather. Unlike the other hardy lilies, it is propagated by seed rather than by root division, and it is rarely offered by nurseries. For tub gardens, the substitute of choice is the sweet little white 'Hermine', discussed below. For small ponds, use the pure white Marliac 'Albida', which, though officially sized as a medium, dwarfs itself in smaller spaces. *N. tetragona* requires full sun.

Yellow
N. tetragona 'Helvola'
ZONES 3–10

This *N. tetragona* hybrid is truly charming in a small water garden. Star-shaped, semidouble blossoms with daintily pointed petals open in the afternoon. The olive-green leaves are mottled purple and brown. 'Helvola' is one of a handful of water lilies that does as well in a pond 12 inches deep or a little less as in the standard depth of 15 to 24 inches. Partial to full sun.

Small (3 to 6 square feet)

Lilies classed as small are adaptable to a tub garden and also may be just right to fill a special niche in a larger pond. Some larger lilies will adapt to small spaces, however, so you can look for suitable plants for tubs and barrels among the larger size categories.

Small, exquisite 'Hermine', an important petite.

White
Nymphaea 'Hermine'
ZONES 3–11

One of the few small white water lilies, 'Hermine' blooms abundantly over a long season from its first year. The classical star shape, golden center, and fresh green lily pads are exquisite, and you can just catch the slight fragrance if you cup a flower in your hand the first day it blooms. 'Hermine' is suited to a tub garden but flourishes in deep ponds as well. Full or partial sun.

'Chromatella'.

Yellow/Bronze

N. 'Chromatella'

ZONES 3–11

Loved for its long season of bloom and generous flowering, this old favorite has luminous canary-yellow petals that cup a core of deep chrome-yellow stamens. When young, the olive-green lily pads are richly mottled in shades of chestnut-maroon. As they age, they change to an even green. Semidouble, 'Chromatella' is classed with both the smalls and the mediums since it will adapt completely to the restrictions of a tub 2 feet across and 12 inches deep or even somewhat smaller. Full or partial sun.

N. 'Paul Hariot'

ZONES 3–11

One of the fascinating group of water lilies known as changeables, 'Paul Hariot' displays that characteristic in its most reliable and dramatic form. A perfect canary yellow at the outset, as the flower matures the shade gradually changes toward bronze-pink and then dark red. The little 4-inch blossoms have a slight fragrance and keep well when cut. The beautifully mottled pads make this changeable very desirable for tubs and small gardens where there's space for only one lily. It was developed by Latour Marliac and named for a French horticultural writer who was his friend. Full or partial sun.

Small-Medium (4 to 12 square feet)

Pink

N. 'Pink Beauty' (formerly N. 'Fabiola')

ZONES 3–11

Highly recommended for a new pond, 'Pink Beauty' blooms over a long season; for years it has been one of the most popular water lilies. The cup-shaped, multipetaled flowers with lush golden centers are beautiful and slightly fragrant. If set out early in the season, the plant often bears two or more blooms at a time even in its first summer. Most other hardy lilies display flowers one by one for the first one or two seasons until the rootstock has developed several crowns. The lily pads are a rich green. 'Pink Beauty' succeeds with as little as 5 inches of water over its crown. Full sun.

N. 'Marliacea Carnea'
ZONES 3–11

This classical, semidouble, cup-shaped water lily with luminous light flesh-pink petals and rose-pink sepals was developed by Latour Marliac. An outstanding feature of 'Carnea' is its ability to bloom in partial sun better than other hardies. Described as small-medium, the plant grows in a tidy clump even in large ponds, and succeeds at any depth from 10 to 36 inches. The flower is fragrant and is good for cutting. Full or partial sun.

Red
N. 'Ellisiana'
ZONES 3–7

Especially pretty in the half-open stage, the buds of 'Ellisiana' become many-petaled red blossoms trimmed in deeper red. This is a delightful small-medium plant that succeeds in tubs and small ponds in the moderate summers of the Pacific Northwest in Zones 3 through 7. Where air temperatures head for the nineties week after week, as in the deep South and the deserts of the Southwest, the petals absorb too much heat and the flowers will actually wilt. Full sun.

N. 'Perry's Dwarf Red'

ZONES 3–11

Hybridizer Perry Slocum considers this to be his outstanding red introduction for tub culture. It produces a profusion of very rich red blossoms with an average of thirty petals each. Full sun.

Medium (6 to 12 square feet)

Many medium lilies will dwarf when they are planted in a small pond.

White

Nymphaea 'Gonnere'

ZONES 3–9

Unique among water lilies, the pure white flowers of 'Gonnere' have oval centers; others have round centers. But its greatest asset is the visibility of its very double blossoms. It has less foliage than other lilies, so the flowers stand out, a welcome feature in a pond that has space for only a few lilies or in a big pond where the individual flower may get lost. A rather shy bloomer, 'Gonnere' is well worth the wait between flowers. Although grouped among the mediums, this is a lily that will scale down to fit a smaller space, and it is first-rate in small ponds. Full sun.

N. 'Marliacea Albida'

ZONES 3–11

For almost a century, this has been a favorite choice of gardeners looking for a pure white water lily that is fragrant and a prolific bloomer. Modest in size, the cup-shaped semidouble flowers sometimes stand slightly erect 1 to 2 inches above deep

The classic white 'Marliacea Albida' will dwarf in a small space. (Photo by Michael Elspas)

green leaves that are tinted red or purple on the undersides. Full sun.

Yellow/Bronze
N. 'Charlene Strawn'
ZONES 3–11

One of the best yellows, 'Charlene Strawn' is recommended because it is naturally eager to bloom. The fragrant flowers are held 1 to 2 inches above the water, which is not typical of hardy lilies. This lily, named for the wife of Dr. Kirk Strawn, blooms over a long season. Full or partial sun.

N. 'Comanche'

Zones 3–11

With its sunrise or sunset colors, 'Comanche' is considered the best of the changeables. The slightly fragrant blossoms open nearly yellow, deepen to rose-apricot, then turn bronze touched with copper. The lily pads are handsomely speckled. This is one of the largest changeables and is a good choice for big ponds. Stimulated by extra fertilizer and plenty of space, it will grow into a very imposing plant. 'Comanche' bears lots of blooms each season, and the flowers are good for cutting. Full or partial sun.

N. 'Joey Tomocik'

Zones 3–11

This bright yellow Kirk Strawn hybrid produces flowers consistently over a long blooming season. The blossoms are held above the water surface and have a spicy fragrance. Full sun.

N. 'Indiana'

Zones 3–11

This changeable changes from bronze burnt-orange tones to a real red on the third or fourth day. The reds of other changeables are softer, not as vibrant. Perfectly adaptable to growing in a tub or a very small pond, 'Indiana' bears simple, pretty little blossoms with big golden centers. It is slightly fragrant. The olive-hued lily pads are mottled with rich purple. Full or partial sun.

N. 'Sioux'

Zones 3–11

Another of the sunny changeables, 'Sioux' is as yellow as 'Comanche' when it opens but tends toward russet red as it matures. The petals are well separated, pointed, and perfectly aligned in a star formation above bronze leaves spotted with brown. It is exceptionally beautiful. Full or partial sun.

Pink

N. 'Firecrest'

ZONES 3–11

This lily is for the pond that already has one of everything usual! The star-shaped semidouble flowers have soft pink petals surrounding glowing red-tipped stamens that stand erect and look like little flames. The leaves are dark green splotched with purple. A sweet, tangy scent haunts the blossoms. 'Fire-

Hardy 'Firecrest' has a flaming center.

crest' opens its first flowers in spring and goes on producing generously until fall. Full sun.

N. 'Masaniello'

ZONES 3–11

Full as a rose and held distinctly above the water, the blossoms of 'Masaniello' have showy rose-pink petals dotted with carmine red. The sepals are white, and the overall color deepens with maturity. This lovely, fragrant water lily is especially valued for its ability to bloom in light shade. Full or partial sun.

N. 'Perry's Fire Opal'

ZONES 3–11

This is the flower for the gardener whose first thought is fragrance. It is very fragrant, especially on the first day of blooming. Backed by handsome lily pads with a bronze cast, the large, cup-shaped flowers are a strong pink. They last well when cut. A wide-spreading plant, 'Perry's Fire Opal' succeeds as well in a small water garden as in a large one. The hybridizer is Perry Slocum. Full sun.

N. 'Pink Sensation'

ZONES 3–11

An outstanding choice for the owner who likes to take tea with the lilies in the late afternoon and wants beautiful flowers to make bouquets. The fragrant blossoms are a sensational light pink with large, elongated oval petals, and they remain open an hour or so later than other water lilies. 'Pink Sensation' comes into bloom early in the summer and flowers generously until late in the season. The hybridizer is Perry Slocum. Full sun.

N. 'Rosy Morn'

ZONES 3–11

'Rosy Morn' scents the garden its first day open and enchants the gardener with lots of elegant, truly superior blossoms. The large, tulip-shaped flowers, with long, pointed, two-toned pink petals, are held above the water on erect stems. This lily is good for cutting. Full sun.

N. 'Sumptuosa'

ZONES 3–8

The double flowers are an unusual deep pink — redder than baby pink. The outer petals shade from pale to light pink, and the inner ones darken to carmine as they approach the crown of golden stamens. It has a light fragrance the first day. This sweet lily performs especially well in the Pacific Northwest. Full sun.

Red

N. 'Sirius'

ZONES 3–11

'Sirius' is a prolific bloomer with more vermilion than red in the petals. The flowers are nicely set off by green leaves interestingly flecked with maroon. It has a slight fragrance. Full or partial sun.

N. 'Splendida'

ZONES 3–11

Planted according to the rules, 'Splendida' rewards the gardener with consistent flowering. Large red petals shaded with white and carmine surround brilliant orange stamens. The overall effect is strawberry red. A slight but sweet fragrance is noticeable as each blossom comes into bloom. Full sun.

N. 'Sultan'

ZONES 3–11

This full, beautiful water lily is a true cherry red, tipped and flecked with pure white. It bears a profusion of flowers that endure soaring temperatures wonderfully well and can be counted on by southern gardeners. The fragrance is slight but pleasant. Full sun.

N. 'Charles de Meurville'

ZONES 3–11

This is the largest and probably the most fragrant of the red-toned lilies. The petals have a touch of white. The scent is sweet and intense the first day. The lily pads are large and a pretty, shiny green. Full sun.

N. 'James Brydon'

ZONES 3–11

A lily with many attributes, 'James Brydon' will bloom lavishly and dependably in a tub 12 inches deep as well as in a pond or lake. The clump is trim and tidy, and once established will bear more than one blossom at a time even the first year, which is not typical of hardy lilies. The fragrant, peonylike flowers are a superb crimson stained with orange, though oddly enough the first several blossoms of the season tend to be a pink-red. This color anomaly recurs after the lily is transplanted. The foliage is a rich dark green. Developed at Dreer Nurseries of Philadelphia around 1900, the lily is named for Henry A. Dreer's client and friend, the head gardener of the Simpson estate. It is most successful in areas that have snow in winter, and/or mild summers as in the Pacific Northwest. Heat over 95 degrees causes some wilting of the petals. Full or partial sun.

'Radiant Red', a belle for the deep South. (Photo by George L. Thomas III)

N. 'Radiant Red'

ZONES 3–11

The truly brilliant crimson flowers are held an inch or so above gracefully arranged lily pads in a beautiful shade of rich green. The blossoms have a slight fragrance. This is one of the few hardy red lilies that produces very well in the deep South, and it blooms over a long season. It flourishes in deep ponds. Full sun.

N. 'William Falconer'

ZONES 3–7

This wonderfully handsome and imposing plant has the darkest red flowers of any of the hardy lilies. The color is enhanced by lily pads that change from maroon to green. It is an excellent bloomer. This lily thrives where summer temperatures are moderate, but the petals will wilt when the temperature exceeds 95 degrees. Full sun.

Medium-Large (6 to 12 square feet or more)

Medium-large lilies will occupy 12 square feet or more, given enough space. Many will adapt to a smaller pond but not to anything as small as a tub garden. None of the hardy lilies are in the large category, covering 12 square feet or more; this size is found only among the tropicals.

White

Nymphaea 'Queen of Whites'

ZONES 3–11

The outstanding cup-shaped, clear white flowers are rather similar to those of 'Marliacea Albida', but they have two to four more broad petals. The medium-size flowers are slightly fragrant and are produced steadily over the entire season. The plant adapts well to deep ponds. Full sun.

N. 'Gladstone'

ZONES 3–11

The cup-shaped flowers of 'Gladstone' have pure white petals surrounding a bright yellow center. The leaf stalk is interestingly striped, and the leaves are a fresh green. It's a robust plant that can adapt to growing in water up to 3 feet deep, but it will stay in a tidy clump even when growing in a lake. The blossoms have a slight fragrance and are excellent for cutting. Full sun.

N. *odorata* var. *gigantea*
Fragrant water lily
ZONES 3–11

One of the most fragrant of all lilies, this North American native has large star-shaped flowers 3 to 5 inches across. When planting, use a bushel or more of soil because it spreads rapidly, becoming root-bound in a 10- to 20-quart container in one season. Full sun.

N. 'Virginalis'
ZONES 3–11

This broad-petaled, showy, very full lily floats serenely on the water. Slightly fragrant and a lavish, dependable bloomer, 'Vir-

'Virginalis'. (Photo by George L. Thomas III)

ginalis' is one of the first to come into flower and one of the very last to go dormant in autumn, adding weeks of flowering to either end of the water garden season. The leaves are dark green on top, while the undersides vary from amber-green to purple-green. The stems of flowers and leaves have a fuzzy coating. The plant thrives in up to 3 feet of water. Full sun.

N. 'Virginia'
ZONES 3–11

Nurseryman Charles B. Thomas named this lily for his mother, Virginia. The blossom is unusually showy out on the pond; it is nearly double, with lots of slightly crimped, long, narrow, elegant petals that give it a full, fluffy look. It has a slight scent. 'Virginia' stays open an hour or so after most other hardies have closed and will succeed at greater depths than the average lily. It is one of the best hardy whites. Full or partial sun.

Yellow
N. 'Sunrise'
ZONES 3–11

The showy, star-shaped, semidouble yellow flowers have long, narrow, somewhat curved petals surrounding an orange-gold heart and look almost fluffy. Like 'Pink Sensation' and 'Virginia', its blooms remain open later in the afternoon than those of most hardy varieties. A slight fragrance is especially noticeable the first day. The stems have an interesting downy covering. Full sun.

N. 'Texas Dawn'
ZONES 5–11

Fragrant, bearing a profusion of large flowers all at one time, this outstanding semidouble golden lily with sunrise-colored

'Sunrise' stays open later than other hardy lilies.

'Texas Dawn' blooms and blooms and blooms.

stamens is becoming one of the most popular lilies, hardy or tropical. Unlike the average hardy water lily, which in the first season puts up one blossom and then rests for several days before putting up another, 'Texas Dawn' doesn't seem to need a rest between flowers. It was introduced in 1990 by Texas hybridizer Kenneth Landon. Its hardiness is presently described as limited to Zones 5–11, but its northern range hasn't been fully tested. The plant is suited to large as well as medium-size ponds. Full or partial sun.

Pink
N. 'Hollandia'
Zones 3–11

Substantial, exquisite, and fully double, 'Hollandia' has pale pink inner petals around a heart of golden stamens, with outer petals bleached almost white. The slightly fragrant flowers, borne in profusion, are good for cutting. There's little mention of 'Hollandia' in the water garden literature before 1988, but it has been around for several decades and is an outstanding, robust lily. It grows as a tidy clump even in large ponds and lakes. Full sun.

N. 'Mayla'
Zones 3–11

The color of the blossoms is remarkable — a rich deep fuchsia, with gold-tipped inner petals that match the golden stamens. This is a big fragrant flower that floats a little above the water and is the center of attention from the moment it starts to open. The lily pads are bronze-maroon. Kirk Strawn developed this lily and first released it in 1993. Full sun.

'Mayla'. (Photo by Kirk Strawn)

N. 'Mrs. C. W. Thomas'
ZONES 3–11

This lily is only for a large pond, where it can spread out. The big, beautiful shell-pink flowers are gifted with a haunting fragrance. It was named for Charles B. Thomas's great-grand-mother and is a choice for collectors. Plant it in a 30-quart or larger container because its rootstock spreads rapidly. Full sun.

N. 'Peter Slocum'
ZONES 3–11

This plant, named for the son of hybridizer Perry Slocum, is an exceptionally large, lovely double lily. The blossom has many beautifully arranged rows of shell-pink petals and a sweet fragrance. The bud is very handsome, and the flowers are excellent for cutting. Full sun.

N. 'Rose Arey Hybrid'
ZONES 3–11

Impatient gardeners love this hybrid variant of 'Rose Arey'. The clear pink flowers come into bloom earlier in the season than others, and they open sooner in the morning. The large, star-shaped, semidouble flowers have a distinct fragrance reminiscent of sweet fennel. Full sun.

N. 'Gloire de Temple-sur-Lot
ZONES 3–11

This is the most double water lily ever. A shy bloomer, 'Gloire' is worth whatever time, patience, and space are required to bring it into bloom. Reminiscent of a centifolia rose, this fragrant, historic lily has golden stamens surrounded by one hundred petals that change from pale pink to cream to white as they age. A hybrid developed by Latour Marliac, it is a superb lily for collectors and is suited to a medium or large pond. Full sun.

N. 'Arc en Ciel'
ZONES 3–11

Exquisite in every detail, this historic Marliac hybrid was named for the rainbow of colors in its blossoms and its magnificently variegated foliage: purple, rose, ivory, pink, yellow, green, and bronze. The slim, delicate, soft pink petals complement the foliage perfectly. Flowering is moderate, but pond owners plant 'Arc en Ciel' for its unique foliage color rather than for its flowers. Full sun.

Red

N. 'Attraction'

ZONES 3–11

The deep garnet-red flower of this Marliac introduction may measure as much as 8 to 10 inches across, making it one of the largest hardy lilies in cultivation. There's a touch of white in the sepals, and the cup-shaped, semidouble flowers are slightly fragrant. 'Attraction' blooms freely even in the hot South. It will adapt to growing in water 3 feet deep or more. Prefers full but tolerates partial sun.

N. 'Escarboucle'

ZONES 3–11

The brilliant red of this spectacular, cup-shaped, double-flowered Marliac lily rivals the color of the cardinal flower and

'Arc en Ciel' and its beautiful lily pads. (Photo by Anita Nelson)

always comes as a surprise. Some water lilies that are called red are somewhat pink, but no one ever was tempted to call this anything but red red. In contrast, the foliage is dark green. The petals are rather pointed, and it is moderately fragrant. It is attractive in large ponds and more successful in deep water than most lilies. Full sun.

Planting, Culture, and Winter Care

If they are set out after the chill of very early spring but before growth gets well under way, most hardy lilies will produce blooms the first summer. Within the frost belt they accept transplanting from early spring through early or midfall, up until a few weeks before the first killing frost. They can be planted year round in Zones 10 and 11. Like many garden flowers, they sulk a bit if they are moved bareroot while they are in bloom.

In spring and summer, nurseries sell water lilies already rooted and growing in containers; mail order houses ship them bareroot and packed in moist materials in a plastic bag. Their arrival is timed for planting in your area, about when water temperatures are 55 to 60 degrees. Hardy water lilies have a knobby rootstock that resembles an iris rhizome. If you can't plant the rhizomes right away, they will keep for several weeks submerged in water in a cool place out of direct sun. Keep them moist or wet and shaded while you prepare to plant.

Hardy water lilies are shallow-rooted: they need space to spread up and out, but not down. Plant the rhizomes in pans 6 to 8 inches deep that hold 9 to 20 or more quarts of soil, the larger the better. Extra growing room encourages the development of multiple crowns. Since each crown sends its blossoms to the surface one at a time at three- to seven-day intervals, the more crowns that develop, the more flowers will pop simultaneously to spread a carpet of color across the water. The largest containers commonly found in aquatic gardens are the 22- to 48-quart tubs for growing three or four plants. Tubs that hold 9 to 10 quarts of soil are the minimum recommended for standard and larger sizes; the smaller lilies need at least a 5-quart container.

Lilies thrive in heavy garden topsoil — clay isn't a negative word here — that has *not* been mixed with manure, mulch, compost, peat moss, or vermiculite. Fill one-third of the container with soil. Set the rhizome on the soil and add more dirt so the crown and its growing tip are barely above the soil. Rhizomes with horizontal growing tips should be planted at a 30-degree angle, with the growing tip uppermost and just above the surface of the soil. Pineapple-like rhizomes are planted upright with the growing tip just breaking the soil surface. Firm the soil around the rhizome.

Except when planting pygmy and small water lilies, space the containers several feet apart in the pond. They need room to spread up and out across the surface. Set the container in the pond with 6 to 18 inches of water over the growing tip. If the rhizome has already developed floating (uncurled) lily pads, position the container at a depth that allows at least a few of them to float on the water. After a two-week period of adjustment, you can expect a just-planted water lily to send up new foliage.

The leaves of the hardy lilies are born and die throughout the growing season. One of the pond owner's few continuing chores is the removal of yellowing foliage. A tool known as a lily pruner makes the job quick and easy. Removing closed four-day-old blossoms makes the pond more tidy and, some say, speeds the rate at which the plant will present new flower buds. Vigorous growers, water lilies multiply quickly in a fertile environment. When the average water temperature is above 75 degrees, the plants will produce more blooms with twice-monthly fertilizing. In the cooler months of the growing season, fertilize monthly, as described in Chapter 5.

Winter Care

In frost-free zones, the hardy lilies tend to slow down a bit, but they continue to grow, as do the tropicals. In the frost belt, the rhizomes of the hardy lilies will live through winter in the pond if they are below pond ice. Their survival is determined by the temperature of the water, not that of the air. Don't judge pond temperatures by the depth of frost in your garden. Cold weather sends frost inches down into the earth far more easily than it can maintain even a thin film of ice on the pond. If the pond water seems likely to freeze down to the water lily containers, lower the pans. If the pond isn't deep enough to escape the ice, move the lilies in their pans to a cool place — a frost-free garage, for instance, or a root cellar. Cover the containers with damp cloths or newspapers, then wrap them in a plastic bag to maintain the moisture. Check the rhizomes now and then to be sure they don't dry out and are safe from rodents.

Dividing Hardy Water Lilies

Hardy water lilies growing in 10-quart or larger containers eventually get root-bound and produce fewer flowers and smaller leaves. This happens after a single season in Zones 8 through 11, and after two or three years elsewhere. Like many land plants, water lilies are renewed by division, and spring is the best time to divide them. But if you don't mind losing several weeks of flowering you can divide hardy lilies any time after the water becomes warm enough to work in (say above 49 degrees) until a month before the first frosts are expected.

The work of dividing rhizomes should be done on a plastic sheet in the shade. Turn the lily container upside down and empty out the contents gently so as not to break any of the growing points. Wash off the roots and study the growing points, mentally dividing the rhizome into 3- to 6-inch sections, each with a healthy crown, or growing tip. The pineapple-type rhizome grows into a forbidding tangle, but if you study it carefully you'll recognize the growing tips by the stubs of the past season's growth that cling to them. With a clean, sharp knife, make the cuts. Plant these pieces the same way the original lily rhizome was planted.

But you can usually get more than just these 3- to 6-inch sections from the crowns. The rhizome also has eyes about the size of the end of your thumb. After identifying the crowns, look for the eyes and cut these out, each with a section of rhizome. Don't impinge on the crown-related division. Plant each eye with its section of rhizome in a 5-inch pan or a full-size container with the growing tip above the soil. (Don't give in to the temptation to plant all the rhizomes and eyes unless you have plenty of pond space or lots of pond-owning friends.) Place the pots containing eye divisions in the pond with 2 or 3 inches of water over the soil. In a week or two the eyes will develop little growths, which are actually curled-up leaves. These will reach up to the surface of the pond and continue to grow. When they are growing strongly, transfer the division to a larger container and place it at a depth that allows at least three pads to float on the surface. The following season it will produce flowers. Occasionally, in a season perfectly suited to water lilies' needs, new plantings from eyes will bloom the first year, but generally they will not. You can plant several pieces of rhizome together to develop for the first season, but as they grow, you will have to separate and repot them in individual containers.

The Best Tropical Lilies

The tropical water lilies are some of the most exquisite and romantic flowers in the world. As a group they do everything on a bigger scale than the hardy lilies. Their blossoms — some nearly a foot across — are held 5 to 10 inches above the water, and they are more likely than the hardy lilies to produce more than one flower at a time. The big, full flower buds rise through the water and open to fill the pond with color all summer long and for weeks after the first chilly weather has wilted the hardies. Tropical lily pads tend to be larger and more structured, and may occupy half again as much surface space as the pads of many of the hardies. Their shapes present endless elegant variations. There are smooth pads, toothed and crimped pads, and fluted pads. In many plants the pads have purple or maroon undersides and are mottled or speckled or splashed in pink, bronze, or deep, vibrant colors that contrast beautifully with the fresh green of the hardy lily pads — a change from the green green of the typical water garden foliage. But on some leaves, no sooner have you begun to study the variegations than they fade, like the grin on Alice's Cheshire cat, leaving only green behind.

The day-bloomers without exception are sweetly fragrant. The night-bloomers have a heavy, pronounced scent unlike anything else, mysterious and compelling — especially on the first evening they open. The perfume is irresistible to night-flying insects. Compelled by one heady scent after another, the insects go from flower to flower and cross-pollinate them all. A night-blooming tropical can take a whole hour to fully open, and watching it happen on a night when the moon is full is as romantic an experience as the garden has to offer. You can actually see the flower bud unfold, as though your personal time machine is standing still. The stars are just beginning to twinkle when the first sepal jerks open, and soon a second slips open, then another. In the moonlight the silky petals of 'Wood's White Knight' gleam against the black water. Then, one by one, the petals open out until you can see the golden stamens at the heart of the blossom.

The pointed petals of the day-blooming tropical lilies glow in shades of magenta, red, pink, white, yellow, rosy yellow, and fabulous shades of blue, violet, and purple. The blues are of such shades that the color isn't easy to capture on film. A scarce star-shaped single lily called 'Green Smoke' shades from chartreuse on the inner petals to light blue-green on the outer ones. The bronze-green leaves have bronze speckling. Because 'Green Smoke' is quite temperamental, it is recommended only for serious collectors. The colors of the night-blooming tropicals are white, pink, and red/magenta, the only colors that can be seen by night-flying insects. Though the colors of some tropicals soften or darken with maturity, none is classed as a changeable.

A few day-blooming tropical water lilies have an extraordinary characteristic: the mature leaves produce plantlets from their center. Plants that put forth new plants in this way are described as viviparous — "vivips" for short. A few kinds will produce vigorous plantlets on every leaf, but others produce sluggish plantlets. 'Dauben', the day-blooming tropical recommended especially for new water gardeners, is the most generous of all the vivips, for it sometimes has two or three generations on the same leaf, one coming out from the other. 'Charles Thomas' is another popular viviparous day-blooming tropical.

Vigorous vivip babies become full-fledged plants in ninety days — over a summer. If you enjoy propagation, cut the babies off and press them into soil in a pan, then set the pans in the pond with a few inches of water over the soil. As they grow, lower the containers deeper into the water so the stems will stretch up, allowing the pads to float.

Tropical water lilies have time to come into bloom even in Zone 3 if they are set out as soon as you receive them. Growers ship tropicals so that they will arrive just as the pond temperature is steadily above 69 degrees. They should begin to bloom after a month or so of temperatures over 80 degrees. In Zone 8 the tropicals typically begin to bloom in May; in Zone 6, in June. However, in regions such as the Pacific Northwest where temperatures do not stay over 80 degrees for at least three or four weeks, tropicals usually will not bloom.

The tropical day-bloomers that have been the most popular over the decades include the beautiful pink 'General Pershing', 'Pink Pearl', and, recently coming on strong, 'Madame Ganna Walska'. Traditionally, the pink tropicals are less popular than the blues because there are lots of lovely hardy pinks but no hardy blues. The point missed is that the pink tropicals will produce many more blooms the first year and will have flowers for several weeks after cold weather has put the hardy pinks to sleep. Among the most popular blues are 'Dauben', 'Blue Beauty', 'Mrs. Martin E. Randig', 'Charles Thomas', and 'Blue Triumph'. White day-bloomers of outstanding merit are 'Marian Strawn' and 'White Delight'.

The preferred night-bloomers are the exquisite 'Wood's White Knight'; huge 'Texas Shell Pink'; lush, double 'Emily Grant Hutchings'; and 'Red Flare'.

Day-Blooming Tropical Water Lilies
Small (up to 6 square feet)

Blue/Violet

Nymphaea colorata

This perfect little wisteria-blue tropical lily with fresh green leaves performs very well even in tubs and kettles with just 6 inches of water over the growing tip. Because the color stays a good blue from the first day to the last, it is preferred by some over the paler 'Dauben', which blooms so surely and lavishly. It readily produces little round tubers toward the end of the growing season. Full or partial sun.

Small-Medium (up to 12 square feet)

White

Nymphaea 'Marian Strawn'

A stately lily, 'Marian Strawn' becomes quite large when it is grown in a large space. The very fragrant, multipetaled white blossoms have buttercup-yellow centers and are held well above the water surface. The plant blooms from morning to late afternoon in summer and early fall, and in frost-free regions it goes on flowering into winter. An almost black green flecks the lily pads, which may be as much as 15 inches in diameter. Kirk Strawn named the lily for his mother. Prefers full sun, but succeeds in partial sun.

Blue/Violet

Nymphaea 'Dauben'

A sweet, soft blue lily that is virtually foolproof and one of the most prolific bloomers, this is the best tropical for the water garden's first year. The plant blooms more readily than other lilies, hardy or tropical, even when given only three or four hours of sunlight. It adapts to the small space of a tub and

'Dauben', a day-blooming tropical for small spaces.

The viviparous foliage of the day-bloomer 'Charles Thomas' produces baby plants.

thrives in very shallow ponds with just 4 inches of water over the container. But if well fertilized and placed in a large pond, 'Dauben' will spread to 3 or 4 feet. A viviparous lily, it produces lots of little piggyback plants complete with foliage and buds. You'll see a leaf with a viviparous plantlet on it and another little plant on the first one with yet another tiny new bud showing. Gardeners who prefer vibrant colors may find this blue, which fades to almost white at maturity, too pale. But as long as it is in still water with warm direct sunlight, it insists on blooming. Full or partial sun.

N. 'Charles Thomas'

This sweetly fragrant periwinkle-blue tropical lily is bluer than 'Dauben' and blooms steadily over a long season. It is not as abundantly viviparous as 'Dauben', bearing plantlets late in the season on spectacularly mottled foliage. 'Charles Thomas' was developed by hybridizer Jack Wood. Don't confuse this with the 'Charles Thomas' lotus. Full or partial sun.

N. 'Robert Strawn'

This is a favorite of water gardeners who want a good cutting flower as well as a showy display in the water garden. The blossoms, a wonderful lavender blue, are held well above the speckled green foliage. Full or partial sun.

N. 'Hilary'

A new, nicely compact lily, 'Hilary' has pointed petals that enhance the star shape of the lovely violet-pink blossoms. Though the plant is classed as small-medium, it grows as well in a tub as it does in a large pond. The viviparous lily pads are attractively speckled. Full or partial sun.

'Madame Ganna Walska', named for the Polish opera singer who created Lotusland, her Santa Barbara home.

N. 'Madame Ganna Walska'

Introduced in 1990, this tropical outblooms all the other pinks. The color is a striking violet-pink, highlighted by strongly mottled emerald-green foliage. It is viviparous and a very prolific bloomer. Opera buffs may recognize the name. A fascinating Polish singer, Madame Walska left Europe in 1941 for California and in Santa Barbara developed water gardens on her estate, Lotusland. The gardens are open to the public on a limited basis. Full or partial sun.

Small-Large (1 to 12 square feet or more)

The two lilies in this size category grow well miniaturized in an 18-inch tub, but given the space will cover more than 12 square feet.

Blue/Violet

Nymphaea 'Panama Pacific'

The flowers, blue-purple with touches of red, are distinguished by the intensity of their color. The viviparous lily pads, speckled maroon-brown, are a bit smaller in relation to the blossoms than those of most other lilies, making a more compact plant. 'Panama Pacific' will adapt to a tub garden but will grow considerably larger in a bigger pond. Its compactness makes it a good variety to plant in a greenhouse pond for winter. Prefers full sun, but succeeds in partial sun.

N. 'Mrs. Martin E. Randig'

This lily is very similar to 'Panama Pacific'. The petals are bluer and edged with a bit of reddish purple, and the sepals are a dark rose pink. The bronzy green lily pads, very viviparous, are small in proportion to the overall plant size. It adapts readily to either a tub or a big pond. The flower is named for

'Golden West' is a day-bloomer that tolerates shadier places though it prefers full sun. (Photo by Bill Heritage)

Erika Randig, wife of the hybridizer Martin Randig. Full or partial sun.

Medium (6 to 12 square feet)

Rosy yellow

Nymphaea 'Golden West'

Not all the rosy yellow water lilies fulfill their promise, but 'Golden West' surely does. The very fragrant salmon pink flowers open to a wonderfully deep apricot with glowing golden stamens. The foliage is a nice forest green mottled with maroon. 'Golden West' blooms well in less sun than most water lilies require. Full or partial sun.

Pink

N. 'Shirley Bryne'

This is a rarity, a viviparous pink water lily. The rich, deep pink petals surround a vivid yellow cup. The plant grows with little care and is a prolific and consistent bloomer, even without full sun. Available only since 1992, it was hybridized by Don Bryne, an aquatic nurseryman in Florida. Full or partial sun.

Blue

N. 'Blue Capensis'

A very good bloomer also known as the cape blue water lily, 'Blue Capensis' bears its star-shaped, semidouble, periwinkle-blue flowers over a long season and without any show of temperament. The large green leaves are splashed with purple beneath. Perhaps not quite as foolproof as 'Dauben', this is nevertheless a tough plant that will produce for you consistently if given a fair portion of what it needs. It is adaptable to a 10-inch-deep water garden and will thrive equally well when adapted to 3 feet of water depth. Full sun.

'Blue Capensis' is a native African species that varies its blue flowers.

'Blue Triumph', an immense water lily. (Photo by Don Bryne)

N. 'Blue Triumph'

The eye-catching, intense blue-purple flowers with brilliant yellow centers and dark stamens sometimes are all of 8 inches across. They stand out beautifully against the emerald-green lily pads. The plant is a prolific bloomer. Full sun.

N. 'Leopardess'

The broad-petaled flowers are a beautiful soft sky blue, but 'Leopardess' is named for the spectacular mottling of the leaves, brown-maroon on green. The plant blooms generously over a long season, and in a sunny greenhouse will continue to bloom in winter. It is especially striking when it has space to stretch out. Full or partial sun.

'Margaret Mary' adapts to small spaces.

N. 'Margaret Mary'

The exquisite star-shaped single flowers resemble the prolific 'Dauben', but the color is a much deeper blue. The plant is a bit larger than 'Dauben', too, but it can adapt to a tub just 2 feet square and will bloom in frost-free situations all year round. The mildly viviparous leaves are dark green above and lightly speckled underneath. It was patented by George L. Thomas, Jr., of Lilypons Water Gardens, and named for his eldest granddaughter. Full or partial sun.

Purple

N. 'Director George T. Moore'

'Director George T. Moore' blooms prolifically.

One of the most prolific bloomers, this has magnificent deep blue flowers with darker stamens and a gold center. In the juvenile stage, the foliage is purple beneath and subtly flecked above — a little dab here and a little dab there. A casual observer might not notice the patterning, but it is one way of

establishing its identity. The leaves tend to be a bit smaller than usual in proportion to the size of the flower, which makes a more compact plant. It is suited to all situations from tubs to large ponds. George T. Moore was a director of the Missouri Botanic Garden in St. Louis. Full or partial sun.

Medium-Large (6 to 12 square feet or more)

Medium-large lilies will grow to occupy 12 square feet or more if enough space is available.

White

Nymphaea 'Mrs. George H. Pring'

The fragrant, star-shaped, semidouble flowers are immense, sometimes nearly 12 inches across, creamy white with a center of white-tipped bright yellow stamens. The huge green leaves are splashed reddish brown above and purple-green on the underside. In spite of its potential size, this versatile lily is suited to a small pond. It is amazing to see it thriving in a tub. It was named by George H. Pring for his wife. Full or partial sun.

N. 'White Delight'

This dynamic lily shows a soft bluish pink at some of the petal tips. Among the largest and most double of all white day-bloomers, the spectacular flowers open to 12 inches in diameter and are even fuller than 'Mrs. George H. Pring'. It was hybridized by Charlie Winch of Australia. The foliage is slightly speckled. Full sun.

Yellow

N. 'Aviator Pring'

This favorite yellow day-blooming tropical produces some of

'Yellow Dazzler' stays open late.

the largest flowers seen among the lilies. The round, semidouble, medium yellow blossoms are held well above the water surface. The green leaves have toothed, wavy edges. George H. Pring named the plant for his son, an aviator lost in World War I. Full sun.

N. 'Yellow Dazzler'

The color of this superb tropical water lily is deeper than that of some of the yellows, which tend to be pale, and it blooms lavishly. The flower remains open flat out until almost dusk above foliage that is a real emerald green speckled with bronze. Full sun.

Rosy Yellow

N. 'Afterglow'

The bold, delicately scented flowers have wide petals that combine pink, cream, and yellow in a subtle, luminous mix. They are excellent for cutting. Flecks or spots of a beautiful pink tint the forest-green foliage. The plant adapts to a tub or a small pond. Full sun.

N. 'Albert Greenberg'

A large, robust plant and a very reliable bloomer, it bears star-shaped flowers that are rose-tinged gold. It thrives in any pond over 4 feet in diameter and is very effective in larger spaces. The tropical lilies go on blooming long after the hardies have started to shut down in fall — and this lily continues to bloom for a couple of weeks after other tropicals have faded away, well past the first frosts. Developed by Dr. Monroe Birdsey, professor of botany at Dade Community College in Miami, Florida, the plant is named for the founder of the Everglades Aquatic Nurseries in Florida, who specialized in aquarium plants. Full or partial sun.

'General Pershing'. (Photo by Geoffrey Dipple)

Pink

N. 'General Pershing'

Considered the loveliest of all the pink tropical day-bloomers, 'General Pershing' has the great added virtue of staying open for more hours than the others. The huge, richly scented double orchid-pink flowers open soon after sunrise and close an hour or two after most other day-bloomers have gone to sleep. In fall they close at dusk, and they produce blooms until late in the season. The foliage is mottled purple tinged with green on top and reddish underneath. A large variety, it adapts to a small pond. Prefers full but succeeds in partial sun.

N. 'Jack Wood'

Distinguished by its color, 'Jack Wood' bears an abundance of rich raspberry-red flowers with buttercup-yellow centers and ruby stamens. Held well above the water's surface, this stunning flower fills the garden with a heady perfume that catches deep in your throat. The foliage is lightly splotched avocado green. Full or partial sun.

N. 'Pink Capensis'

Sweetly scented luminous rose-pink flowers are borne all season long by this easy-to-grow, prolific bloomer. The big green lily pads are speckled. Both this pink variety and the blue variety, *N. capensis*, produce fertile seeds that sprout and grow when handled as recommended in Chapter 8 for lotus seed after filing. The seedlings will not necessarily duplicate the parent plant, but they may be close. Full sun.

N. 'Pink Pearl'

If you are looking for a silvery pink day-bloomer for a small water garden, this is the best choice. Very compact, it bears the softest pink flowers of any tropical. A strong bloomer that is classed as small-medium, it becomes medium-large if given space and fertilizer. The foliage is a fresh green. Full or partial sun.

N. 'Pink Perfection'

Among big pinks, 'General Pershing' is the most outstanding, but this very fragrant strong bloomer, with its rose-pink flowers and pink-tipped stamens, comes close. The large lily pads are strongly mottled in reddish brown and green. It works well in ponds from 10 inches to 3 feet deep. Full or partial sun.

N. 'Mrs. C. W. Ward'

Full, fragrant, extraordinarily beautiful pink flowers rise to 12 or more inches above the large, light green lily pads. In frost-free climates it will bloom from April until the winter holiday season. Sold in some catalogs under the name Pink Star, this is one of a group of tropicals called the star lilies for their stellar qualities. Something of a space eater, it spreads its leaves way out and is suited only to a large pond. It is good for cutting. Full sun.

Blue

N. 'Blue Beauty'

A prolific bloomer and classed with 'Director George T. Moore' as the best of the blues, this is our favorite. Intoxicatingly fragrant and illumined by a core of golden stamens and violet anthers, the star-shaped, semidouble flowers rise to 8 inches above the water. With ample space and fertilizing, they may reach 12 inches across. They bloom early, the first day showing a blue as blue as an October sky and deepening toward the center. Short vertical black lines give the buds beauty and distinction. The juvenile lily pads are speckled chestnut, and as they spread out toward the perimeter the speckling fades, leaving dark green above and purplish green underneath. Given plenty of fertilizer and space, the pads sometimes grow to 18 inches in diameter. The plant will thrive in a tub or a pond and in water deeper than most lilies accept. Full or partial sun.

N. 'Wood's Blue Goddess'

A 1990 introduction, this water lily has big blossoms of a light sky blue with a touch of wisteria's lavender, centered by un-

'Wood's Blue Goddess', a lovely day-bloomer. (Photo by Kenny Kirkland)

usual dark purple stamens. The blooms remain open until late in the afternoon. This Jack Wood hybrid is a prolific bloomer that backs its flowers handsomely with speckled green lily pads. The seeds are fertile. Full sun.

Large (12 square feet or more)

Medium-large lilies will shrink or stretch according to the surrounding space and conditions, but the lone entry classed as large needs a full 12 square feet or more in which to develop.

Nymphaea 'Blue Star'

The pointed, star-shaped flower is slightly darker than 'Blue Beauty' and has fewer petals. 'Blue Star' tends to show more water between individual pads than other lilies. The opposite of a compact, it spreads out and stages a spectacular display in a pond that provides plenty of space. Full sun.

Night-Blooming Tropicals
Medium-Large (6 to 12 square feet)

Medium-large lilies will grow to occupy 12 square feet or more if given enough space.

White
Nymphaea 'Missouri'

The matte white flowers are immense, sometimes 12 inches in diameter. The new leaves have a bronze cast, which changes as they grow to very deep green. The mature leaves are distinctly fluted, allowing water to reach halfway to the leaf's center. In a greenhouse pond in winter the plant may produce a few flowers. Full sun.

'Wood's White Knight' blooms at night.

N. 'Wood's White Knight'

This exceptionally beautiful water lily embodies the romance of a water garden by moonlight. The large, star-shaped, semidouble flowers are a creamy white centered by soft yellow-tipped stamens. The emerald-green leaves are scalloped and variegated a darker green on the undersides. A prolific bloomer more compact than other night-blooming whites, it maintains a tidy clump even in a large pond. Full or partial sun.

Rose/Red
N. 'Emily Grant Hutchings'

Everyone has success with this prolific bloomer. The flowers, often produced in clusters, are among the largest water lilies and as sure as any to bloom. Star-shaped and semidouble, they have slightly curved pink-coral petals that look frosted as the color lightens toward the center. The lily pads, small for a night-bloomer, are green with a bronzy red overlay. The plant can bloom in a greenhouse pond in winter. George H. Pring developed this one and named it for the wife of a close St. Louis friend. Prefers full but succeeds in partial sun.

'Emily Grant Hutchings', a night-
bloomer. (Photo by Perry Slocum)

'Texas Shell Pink', a night-bloomer. (Photo by Rolf Nelson)

Pink

N. 'Mrs. George Hitchcock'

This large-flowered soft pink water lily and 'Texas Shell Pink' are the two most beautiful pink night-blooming tropicals. A major difference between them is the narrowness of the petals of 'Mrs. George Hitchcock'. Up to 12 inches in diameter, and backed by coppery green foliage flecked with a darker green, the flowers bloom reliably throughout the summer and continue until late in the season. The plant can bloom in winter in a greenhouse pond. This is another George H. Pring hybrid. Full sun.

N. 'Texas Shell Pink'

A pretty seashell-pink water lily frosted with a lighter pink, it has broad petals, a golden heart, and olive-green foliage, and bears a profusion of flowers. This lovely night-blooming tropical lily, developed from the prolific 'Emily Grant Hutchings' and reliable 'Mrs. George Hitchcock', was introduced in 1980 by the Lilypons Water Gardens in Brookshire, Texas, under the direction of Rolf Nelson. It is extremely dependable. Prefers full but succeeds in partial sun.

Red

N. 'Red Flare'

One of the largest of all water lilies, 'Red Flare' lifts vivid, almost neon, rosy red flowers with deep maroon stamens high out of the water. The narrow-petaled form is distinctive. You can count on loads of flowers, delicious fragrance, and a red you can see in the moonlight. Foliage that is really maroon matches the flowers' maroon stems, and sets off the blossoms beautifully. 'Red Flare' is one of a handful of lilies that will bloom reliably in a greenhouse pond in winter. Full sun.

'Maroon Beauty' and 'Wood's White Knight' perfume the night. (Photo by Ronnie and Jeannie Luttrell)

N. 'Maroon Beauty'

More maroon than red, with a dark red center, and gifted with a compelling fragrance, this lily is smaller than the other good night-blooming reds, 'Red Flare' and 'H. C. Haarstick'. The foliage is a rich bronze-red when young and gets greener as it matures. The hybridizer was Perry Slocum. Full sun.

Large (12 square feet or more)

Red

Nymphaea 'H. C. Haarstick'

For lots of showy, very large, deep carmine-red blossoms, choose this beauty, which has all the intensity of color of 'Red Flare' but is a few shades darker. The flowers, 10 to 12 inches

A wide-angle lens captures the romance of night-blooming tropical lilies in the early morning at Kenilworth Aquatic Gardens, a public park in Washington, D.C., maintained by the National Park Service. (Photo by Adri de Groot)

you set out garden annuals. The plants, shipped bareroot, will arrive leafed out and perhaps budded. They should be planted at once. Unlike the hardy lilies, they will not keep for more than a few days.

Plant them in 10-quart pans or, better yet, in 15- or 20-quart tubs. Tropicals grow with 6 to 18 inches of water over the growing tip, though some, as indicated earlier in this chapter, prefer quite a bit less. About two weeks after they have been planted, the tropicals usually start to grow, and they will begin to bloom in two to four weeks more, depending on the state of the lily when planted and on the weather. You should groom fading foliage as you do for hardy lilies, and fertilize the plants twice a month as long as the temperature of the water is 75 degrees or higher.

At the time when repeated frosts destroy tuberous begonias and caladiums, any tropicals remaining in the pond will die. Most pond owners leave them to die, but you can continue them for next year in a greenhouse pond in full sun. Before frost, lift the plants, trim back the foliage, and place the con-

tainers in the greenhouse pond. The plants will be smaller than in the water garden, but they will continue some growth through the winter, and a few will even bloom. In spring, when the water temperature outside is steadily above 69 degrees, lift and groom the plants, repot them in fresh, fertilized soil, and return the containers to the pond.

Another way to continue a tropical over the winter is to store the clean tuber in distilled water. A week or two after a killing frost, lift the rootstock and wash off as much soil as you can. Pluck off one or more tubers, and air-dry them at room temperature for two days, then remove all the remaining soil and old root fragments. Store the tubers in jars of distilled water, and keep them in a cool closet or cupboard. A temperature of 55 degrees is best. Two months before the pond water temperature will reach 70 degrees, set the tubers to sprout in a pan of water in a sunny window. When the pond temperature maintains a minimum 69 degrees, replant the tubers and return them to the pond. They will come into bloom two to three months later.

7 🐚 The Small Floating-leaved Plants

THE LACY FRILLS of the small floating-leaved plants make a nice contrast with the big round lily pads and the lotus. Most of these plants are rooted in containers, but a few grow free on the surface. They leaf out with the water lilies, sketching fanciful, rather busy, horizontal patterns, each with a distinct texture and form. Some bear sweet little flowers, and a few are truly fragrant. Include a couple in your water garden and they will come to fill a place in your thoughts comparable to the niche occupied by pansies. It is a joy to monitor their meanderings. Not essential, but interesting, dainty, and delightful, they add visual appeal to the plant mix, and help the overall balance of the pond by providing shade and taking nutrients from the drifting algae.

There are tender perennials among the small floating-leaved plants that produce very generously. The hardy perennials will need another season or two to catch up with their productivity, but then they may produce more than you know what to do with, so don't overstock. Aquatic plants like to do things in a big way and quickly.

Myriophyllum aquaticum, parrot's feather, trails leafy stems along the surface of the water between the water lilies. The marginal plants include feathery umbrella palm, pickerel rush, and a small cattail. (Photo courtesy of L. Albee, Longwood Gardens)

And therein lies the caveat about the small floating-leaved plants: some grow so rapidly that they can overwhelm your pond. In some southern states water hyacinth and water lettuce, two of the best plants for clearing up water, are illegal because they have clogged public waterways. When you see a water garden overrun by small green foliage, chances are the floating-leaved plants were left to their own devices and proceeded, as they do, to fill all the space they could. Fortunately, it is easy to remove excess growth from a garden pond.

The Best Small Floating-leaved Plants

Before planting any of these, check local, state, and federal laws: the restrictions are impossible to guess at. Water lettuce and water hyacinth are outlawed in some states where the plants may survive the winter, and federal law prohibits commercial interstate shipment of water hyacinth regardless of climate.

If your interest is primarily flowers, plant water poppies, floating-heart, and the white or yellow snowflakes. The plants are presented in alphabetical order.

Aponogeton distachyus
Water hawthorn
ZONES 8–11

Plant this for the strong, sweet vanilla fragrance of the little white flowers. They rise early in the season and stand an inch or so above the water before almost anything else colors in spring. Flowering ceases in summer but comes back in the fall. The distinctive leaves are elongated dark green ovals about 6 inches long. Water hawthorn is outstanding in cool, clear water, especially on the West Coast from San Diego to Seattle, but will burn up in summer heat that is steadily in the 80s or above.

Culture: Plant in spring with 3 to 8 inches of water over the crown in full sun or partial shade. Once established, water hawthorn gradually adapts to water up to 3 feet deep. It is grown as an annual in regions cooler than Zone 8.

Ceratopteris pteridoides
Floating fern
ZONES 6–11

A beautiful little aquatic fern, this is grown as an annual in Zone 6 and northward. The spore-bearing fronds are usually erect and can grow to be 18 inches long; the fronds that float are about 10 inches long and are sterile. In water that is about 70 degrees, plantlets form along the edges of the triangular leaves, and these propagate. The plant is a lovely addition to the water garden, but it doesn't travel well, so look for it at a local nursery or beg some from a friend.

Culture: Place the plant upon the water and let it float free on the surface. Or press the root tips into a pan of garden soil covered with ½ inch of gravel and set the container in the pond with 3 to 12 inches of water over the crown. Full or partial sun.

Eichhornia crassipes
Water hyacinth
ZONES 8–11

Although water hyacinth is a lovely flowering aquatic and very effective in keeping water clear, it is controlled by various state and federal laws. A single plant does the work of about six bunches of submerged plants. The fine feathery roots, which provide an excellent environment for spawning fish, dangle in the water held by glossy green leaves whose petioles are filled with air. The plants spread rapidly during warm weather and clog waterways if they escape into the wild. The flowers are showy, upright violet-blue spikes that stand about 4 to 9 inches high in a thicket of foliage; they open and close during the daytime for two days before fading away. (Each floret in a spike opens only for a single day.) The flowers are most plentiful when the plants are crowded in an area rich in nutrients. A demonstration of that characteristic makes an interesting project for a youngster. Punch small holes in a shallow pan, half fill it with heavy garden soil, and float half a dozen plants in it in the pond. As the water hyacinths multiply on the nutrients in the soil and water, they will crowd against the container walls and all the plants will bloom together.

Culture: To plant water hyacinth, simply drop it into the water. If the plant falls upside down, it will right itself before it hits the surface. The plant floats on the surface, dangles its roots in the water, and holds the foliage in the air. The plant is so resourceful that if it is upside down in the water, it will invert its foliage and start to grow up while the rootlets start to grow down. To control growth, remove excess plants from the pond and compost them. Don't flush water hyacinth into the sewer system, and don't put it in the garbage. It thrives in sun but will tolerate considerable shade.

Hydrocleys nymphoides
Water poppy
ZONES 9–11

This is one of the prettiest small aquatics. It floats a forest of trim oval green leaves and throughout the season produces

Hydrocleys nymphoides,
water poppy.

three-petaled, 2- to 2½-inch lemon-yellow blossoms centered by chocolate-colored stamens. Pick a water poppy and put your nose right into the flower, you'll notice a slight sweet scent. Cut back and grown in a little water in an aquarium in a sunny window, the plant will winter over and may even bloom a bit.

Culture: When the minimum water temperature is 70 degrees, plant with 4 to 12 inches of water over the crown. A tropical perennial from Brazil, it is grown as an annual in regions cooler than Zone 9. Full or partial sun.

Ludwigia, a small floating-leaved plant with intricate, diamond-shaped foliage, and water lilies at Longwood Gardens. In the background are the purple blooms of Brazilian pickerel rush, hybrid Longwood canna, and, far right, lotus. (Photo courtesy of L. Albee, Longwood Gardens)

Ludwigia sedioides
Ludwigia
ZONE 11

The fascinating aspect of this plant is the foliage, though the flowers are also attractive. Dainty diamond-shaped leaves radiate outward on fine reddish stems, spreading an exquisite green mosaic of foliage across the surface of the water. Small, bright yellow flowers are borne in the axils of the leaves, followed by capsular fruits.

Culture: Plant in spring or summer with 4 to 12 inches of water over the crown in full or partial sun. Ludwigia is hardy as a perennial in Zone 11 and is grown as an annual in cooler regions. There hasn't been enough testing to be certain about its winter hardiness in regions cooler than Zone 11.

Lysimachia nummularia
Creeping Jennie
ZONES 3–8

A vigorous low-growing perennial 1 to 2 inches high with round, dark green leaves, it bears lots of small, cup-shaped, bright yellow flowers in summer. *L. n.* 'Aurea', an attractive golden-leaved form, likes to have wet feet too.

Culture: Plant from spring to fall in heavy garden topsoil. Set in the pond with 1 inch of water over the crown. It thrives in sun, partial sun, or light shade.

Marsilea mutica, *water clover.*

Marsilea mutica
Four-leaf water clover
ZONES 6–11

This dainty and always popular little plant is shaped like its namesake, four-leaf clover. It is a primitive, very ancient fern that floats four-part, cloverlike leaves, 3 inches long, over the water. Strikingly patterned yellow to brown, the foliage presents a delightful contrast to the big smooth pads of the water lilies. This plant occasionally is misidentified and sold under the name *M. quadrifolia,* the smaller European water clover, which is also available from aquatic nurseries, but *M. mutica*'s colorful leaves are the show-stopper.

Culture: In spring or summer, plant with 3 to 12 inches of water over the crown in full or partial sun or partial shade.

Parrot's feather close up.

Myriophyllum aquaticum
Parrot's feather
Zones 6–11

Fast-growing parrot's feather is a handsome ornamental grown for the trailing stems, which can be trained to cascade over the side of a kettle or a waterfall. The plants develop in an interesting way. As the stems rise from their underwater container toward the surface of the pond, they develop sparse, hairlike leaves. Then, as the stems reach the air, the leaves begin to grow in dense whorls, and trailing silvery blue or lime-green "feathers" stretch out over the water. Its surface growth and the leaves, which open and close daily, distinguish this species from the *Myriophyllum* species recommended among the submerged plants in Chapter 5.

Culture: Parrot's feather is sold in bunches of cuttings. Plant them as described for the submerged plants in Chapter 5. Set the container in the pond with 3 to 12 inches of water over the soil. Full or partial sun or light shade.

Nymphoides
Some of the prettiest flowering perennials belong to this genus. The leaves are shaped like miniature lily pads, and here and there a flowering node puts forth three or more slender stems bearing dainty little five-petaled blossoms that open in the morning and last only for a day. Because the plants develop rapidly, propagating them makes an interesting water garden project for a child. Take a stem cutting that includes a sprouted rootlet. Plant it in at least 3 inches of soil covered with ½ inch of rinsed gravel in a pan 4 or 5 inches deep, and about 18 inches long. Place the pan in a sunny spot in the pond with 3 to 4 inches of water over the gravel. By the end of the first

Nymphoides cristata, *white snowflake. (Photo by Elvin McDonald)*

week, new leaves should develop, and by the third or fourth week look for flower buds to develop.

Culture: Where they are hardy, the *Nymphoides* species that follow may be set in the pond any time from spring to fall in full or partial sun with 3 to 12 inches of water over the crown. Hardiness is listed for each species.

N. crenata

Yellow snowflake

ZONES 7–11

The floating chocolate-brown leaves of this species are beautifully patterned with green veins. From spring through fall it bears bright yellow flowers with a vertical wing on each petal.

N. crenata variant

Orange snowflake

ZONES 9–11

Relatively new to America, this is an orange-flowering plant from Australia. In areas cooler than Zone 9 it is grown as an annual.

N. cristata

White snowflake

ZONES 7–11

The sweetly fragrant flowers are ¾ inch across and centered by yellow stamens. They bloom abundantly from spring to fall. Some people know this plant as water snowflake.

N. peltata

Yellow floating-heart

ZONES 5 OR 6–11

The leaves, green and maroon with mottled margins, are 3 to 4 inches in diameter. It is also known as water-fringe because of the charming little bright yellow flowers with a fringe all around that pop open in spring and summer. Plant it with 4 to 12 inches of water over the crown.

Pistia stratiotes

Water lettuce

ZONES 9–11

Water lettuce, like water hyacinth, is a first-rate water-clearer whose uncontrollable perennial growth has made possession of it illegal in some southern states. A floating plant, it produces crowds of leafy rosettes rather like loose, 4-inch-high heads of lettuce. The trailing roots hang down several inches. Miniatures develop around the base of each rosette: pinched off and

Nymphoides crenata, yellow snowflake, with the brilliant red hardy water lily 'Escarboucle'. Like the other cultivated Nymphoides, it opens with the water lilies and closes a little earlier.

floated, these will grow into plants. Now and then a few tiny, greenish flowers appear.

Culture: When the water temperature has stabilized at above 69 degrees, just drop water lettuce into the pond and let it drift with the wind. Like the tropical water lilies, it tolerates water that gradually cools in the fall. When plants accustomed to nursery greenhouse conditions are first introduced outdoors, they start best if shaded from the afternoon sun.

Planting, Culture, and Winter Care

The small floating-leaved plants that are hardy may be set out as soon as the pond water reaches about 50 degrees or above. Annuals and tender perennials are set out when the water temperature stays above 69 degrees. Suppliers will ship plants when it is time to set them out in your area. Open the bags as soon as they arrive, and float on the pond the plants that live on the surface, such as water hyacinth and water lettuce. Following the recommendations in Chapter 5, plant the soil-rooted floating-leaved plants one or two to a 3- or 4-quart pan or small pail. Or, for a quick effect, plant three or four together in 5- to 10-quart containers.

If the plants arrive before your pond has reached the right temperature, keep them indoors in a container of water until the pond is warm enough for planting.

The major maintenance chore is checking the growth of these busily spreading plants. Trimming a floating-leaved aquatic is merely a matter of pinching the stems off at any point. Pull up everything growing beyond where you want it and discard it all on the compost pile. Remove yellowing foliage. Once each month during the growing season, press water lily fertilizer tablets into each plant container as directed on the label. Do not fertilize the submerged plants.

In frost-free areas these perennials will keep right on growing. In the frost belt the small floating-leaved hardy perennials shut down after repeated frosts. The tender perennials should be discarded. Cut back the perennials that are hardy in your area and lower the containers to positions that will not be reached by ice. If that isn't possible, store them for the winter as suggested in Chapter 6 for water lilies.

8 ⟨❧⟩ The Sacred Lotus and Other Nelumbos

THE LOTUS IS THE WATER GARDEN'S most fascinating plant. It is ordinary for a lotus to be extraordinary. The large pointed bud rises on a stem 2 to 6 feet tall and unfolds a full, gorgeous flower not unlike a water lily. When the flower is completely open it is as big around as a person's face and exotically, sometimes powerfully, perfumed. The colors are lush shades with combinations of white, pink, red, yellow, and cream. For three days the blossom opens in the morning before the water lilies, and on two days it closes by midafternoon. On the third day the petals begin to fall, leaving a seedpod that looks like the spout of a watering can. A few exceptional cultivars like 'Momo Botan' hold their petals for up to six days. The seedpod is yellow when the lotus first opens, then becomes flushed with green until it is all green. After the petals fall, the pod expands until it has doubled in diameter and over a period of six weeks or so turns from green to brown. That's harvest time for those who air-dry these seedpods for winter arrangements. When it has matured, the seedpod makes a U-turn and heads for the water to make more lotus.

The blossoms of 'Mrs. Perry D. Slocum', when fully open, are as big around as a person's head, on stems 2 to 6 feet tall. (Photo by George L. Thomas III)

Amazing though the flower is, its exotic foliage is enough to recommend it. Two or three weeks after being planted in midspring, a lotus tuber sends up floating leaves, which look something like enormous lily pads without the notch or slit. Then curled-up aerial leaves rise, to unfurl high above the water. These are shaped like wide, very shallow bowls or inverted parasols. When the morning breeze stirs the lotus stems, drops of dew roll around on the aerial leaves and shine like diamonds in the sunlight. The leaves hold rain for hours after a shower. The aerial leaves become dense, creating a sun block for the fish, which love shaded hiding places, and for sun-dependent algae, which do not. The leaves of miniature lotus are 6 to 16 inches across on stems 2 to 3 feet long; large lotus leaves may be 2 feet wide and the height of a tall person — 6 feet. A large pond filled with lotus in full bloom is an unforgettable sight.

A lotus takes as much pond space as a large water lily and requires a bit more care and patience to establish. But the first time you see those exotic aerial leaves and huge flowers materialize out of an early morning mist you will be glad you made the effort to include a lotus in your water garden. More than one lotus plant can overpower a small pond. Many lilies seem almost elastic in their response to the size of their water gardens, but most lotus stay closer to their standard size. An excellent choice for a new, average-size (10 by 10 feet) water garden is the miniature tulip lotus. In a tub it dwarfs somewhat, but it doesn't get much bigger even when it is given a larger space. For a large pond a thrilling combination is lotus 'Mrs. Perry D. Slocum' with water lilies 'James Brydon', 'Virginalis', 'Blue Beauty', 'Pink Sensation', and 'Red Flare'. For foliage contrast include the tiny water clover, *Marsilea mutica,* and for

Lotus leaves soar above a small water garden. Though no buds are visible, the development of elevated foliage is a sign that the huge blossoms are on their way. The white flowers in the foreground are arrowhead, Sagittaria latifolia.

A 6-foot stand of elevated lotus foliage at Longwood Gardens. Lotus also produce floating leaves that resemble lily pads. (Photo courtesy of L. Albee, Longwood Gardens)

contrast in form, plant linear marginals such as water canna, *Thalia dealbata,* and the big narrow-leaved cattail, *Typha angustifolia.*

A common misconception about lotus is that they are frost-tender tropicals. Lotus do thrive in warm climates. They require three to four weeks of temperatures above 80 degrees to bloom, and they thrive in the wild in the Gulf states, the

Atlantic coastal states north to New York, and the Mississippi Valley. In Zone 8 they bloom in June, pause as heat bears down, and resume briefly in September. But the same plants that flower well in the tropics or at the equator are adaptable enough to be perennial in Madison, Wisconsin, Zone 4. Stands of native lotus in frosty Minnesota winter well under the ice. In Zone 6 lotus bloom in mid-July; farther north, in late July. Sun and heat are the keys to flowering — lotus do not bloom well, if at all, in the cloudy, cool Pacific Northwest, though they are grown in water gardens there for the exotic foliage.

Several weeks of sun with temperatures in the eighties will sometimes bring newly planted lotus into bloom the first season. More commonly, after transplanting they produce their first blossoms the second summer. They produce one growing tip per tuber, one flower at a time per joint, though not every joint produces a flower. In its second year the plant will bear many more flowers.

Cutting Lotus Flowers

One or more lotus in a clear crystal vase make a stunning bouquet. In the early morning locate the biggest of the buds that are slow in opening. Those are the first-day blossoms, and they will last longer. The older flowers open first in the morning and unfold more quickly and more fully, but they won't last as long as the new flowers. Cut 14-inch stems and immediately place them in a narrow, 12-inch-high cylinder full of water. The stems are as rigid as sticks when you cut them, but they droop in just a few minutes unless they are placed in water and supported to within a few inches of the bottoms of the blossoms. Keep them away from drafts from an open window, air conditioner, or fan. A cut lotus will last three days. The fragrance is most intense the first day.

Tulip lotus is preferred for small ponds. (Photo courtesy of Perry Slocum)

The Best Lotus Varieties

Lotus is one of the common names for plants of the genus *Nelumbo*. The Latin names may seem harder to remember, but common names often are inaccurate and misleading. The Egyptians had different words for lotus and water lily, but the Romans, who first brought a knowledge of lotus to Europe, used the same name for both plants and we have inherited the Roman confusion. You will look in vain among the *Nelumbos* for the Egyptian white lotus, *Nymphaea lotus*. It is a night-blooming tropical water lily, not a day-blooming lotus. The blue lotus of the Nile, or Egyptian lotus, *Nymphaea caerulea,* is a day-blooming blue tropical water lily.

Many modern lotus are derived from the large, very fragrant pink, rose, or white East Indian lotus, *Nelumbo nucifera*. This is the sacred lotus revered by Buddhists. Our best hardy lotus hybrid, 'Mrs. Perry D. Slocum', is the result of a cross between *N. nucifera* 'Roseum Plenum' and our only native American lotus, the very hardy yellow-flowered *N. lutea*. Like the sacred lotus, *N. lutea* has been an important food source, and one of its common names, pond nuts, reflects that. In spring the casual observer of certain small lakes and big ponds from southern Ontario to Florida and from Minnesota to Texas may spot the high-rise lotus leaves reaching for the sky but will miss the big leaves floating down below and not realize that this is a young forest of native lotus. *N. lutea* flowers are large, and their gold mingles with pink in hybrids like 'Mrs. Perry D. Slocum'. Perry Slocum, who also developed the much-loved hardy water lily 'Pink Sensation', has been the most active hybridizer of *Nelumbo*.

Miniature (up to 6 square feet)

Nelumbo Tulip lotus

ZONES 4–11

The best lotus for tubs and other small water gardens, this plant has pure white tulip-shaped flowers on stems 18 to 24 inches high. The aerial leaves are about the same height. This superb Japanese miniature is known in its homeland as 'Shirokunshi'.

N. 'Momo Botan Minima'

ZONES 4–11

A wonderful deep rose dwarf with a double flower that shades to white on the third day and has a golden center. In a tub the leaves are just 12 inches in diameter; in a pond they are larger and spread out more. Perfect for tubs and ponds, the plant is so much in demand it often is hard to find.

Small-Medium (up to 12 square feet)
Nelumbo 'Charles Thomas'
Zones 4–11

This is the only pink lotus that has a hint of blue or lavender. Other pinks have some yellow or are shades between white and red. It is well suited to barrels and tubs and is very showy growing in a small to medium pond. Perry Slocum, the hybridizer, received for it the first lotus plant patent ever awarded in the United States.

N. 'Chawan Basu'
Zones 4–11

The flowers of this small, beautiful Japanese lotus are cream pink, with each petal tipped or edged in a deeper shade of pink. It performs very well in tub and kettle gardens and is especially attractive combined with the white tulip lotus and the rosy red 'Momo Botan'.

'Charles Thomas' is an adaptable lotus. (Photo by George L. Thomas III)

The huge blooms of 'Roseum Plenum'. (Photo by George L. Thomas III)

N. 'Momo Botan'
ZONES 4–11

A deep rosy red lotus with double blossoms that open and close for up to seven days. It requires several weeks of temperatures in the eighties to come into bloom.

Medium (6 to 12 square feet)

Nelumbo 'Roseum Plenum'
ZONES 4–11

The beautiful rosy pink double flowers open 10 to 12 inches across. The pink is suffused with a little more white each day, but unlike the changeable 'Mrs. Perry D. Slocum', 'Roseum Plenum' doesn't show yellow in the petals. It is easy to grow, flowers freely, and seems to handle cold winters very well.

Medium-Large (6 to over 12 square feet)

All medium-large lotus will grow to occupy 12 square feet of space or more.

'Alba Grandiflora' close up.
(Photo by George L. Thomas III)

Nelumbo 'Alba Grandiflora'

ZONES 4–11

A stunning single-flowered lotus, 'Alba Grandiflora' has pure white petals, a frilly golden heart, great fragrance, and deep green leaves. The blossom is as large as those of the large lotuses, but the stalk is a good 12 inches shorter, making it better proportioned for a tub garden or small pond. A disadvantage is that many of the leaves are higher than the blossoms.

N. lutea

American lotus

ZONES 4–11

The American lotus is also known as water chinquapin, yan-quapin, wonquakin, yellow lotus, and pond nuts. It has creamy

This 'Alba Grandiflora' blossom shows the lotus seed head as it appears during flowering. The seed head to the right has lost its petals and begun to enlarge. (Photo courtesy of Perry Slocum)

'Mrs. Perry D. Slocum' up close.
(Photo by George L. Thomas III)

yellow petals, and once established in a large pond, it is practically indestructible. *N. lutea* is very hardy and especially lovely planted with any pink lotus. Round seeds distinguish it from the Asian sacred lotus, which has elliptical or oval seeds. This would be the only appropriate lotus for a garden of native American plants.

Large (12 square feet or more)

Nelumbo 'Mrs. Perry D. Slocum'
ZONES 4–11

America's best-known and most popular lotus, this exquisite modern hybrid has very large double flowers that start out rosy red, change on the second day to the color of the 'Peace' rose — rosy pink mixed with yellow — and on the third day become creamy yellow white. The stamens are a glowing golden yellow. The leaves are 20 inches in diameter, dramatic in a small pond, and extraordinary when the plant is encouraged to spread over a large pond. This often is the first lotus to begin flowering and the last to stop.

N. 'Red Lotus'
ZONES 4–11

The large-petaled, single, deep rosy red flowers of this lotus contrast beautifully with the deep green foliage. This is the deepest red lotus there is, and it is showy, but if space is limited, the many double blooms of 'Mrs. Perry D. Slocum' will give more satisfaction.

N. nucifera
Sacred lotus, East Indian lotus
ZONES 4–11

This is the lovely light pink single lotus celebrated in Oriental art. It is recommended for beginners because it comes close to delivering everything a lotus promises and stands more adversity than most.

Planting, Culture, and Winter Care

Lotus tubers are shipped bareroot in plastic bags containing moist materials. They are almost as easy to grow as water lilies, but they can be transplanted only during the few weeks in spring when the rootstock is in tuber form. Soon the rootstock is all runners, the tubers atrophy, and transplanting is virtually impossible. During the late summer or fall the runners form tubers; the following spring you can divide and plant them.

A lotus tuber is banana-shaped, usually 6 to 18 inches long, and is set out in water whose temperature is in the forties or fifties or above. It is planted in much the same way as a hardy water lily, but each tuber requires a soil container 16 inches or more in diameter and 9 to 10 inches deep. Miniature varieties require containers about half this size. Plant the tuber with 2 inches of water over the soil, with the top ½ inch of the growing tip above the soil. Cover the soil (but not the growing tip) with ½ inch of rinsed gravel. Handle with care! The tubers and the growing tips are brittle and fragile. Most failures with lotus occur because the growing tip is damaged.

Lotus require at least five to six hours of sun — anything less stunts the foliage. Lotus once were planted with about a foot of water over the tuber, but now they are planted with just 2 to 3 inches over the growing tip. Years of experience at Lilypons Water Gardens has shown that in shallow water the plants are far more productive, especially their first year in the pond.

Throughout the growing season, remove yellowing foliage and spent blossoms. Fertilize the containers with water lily pellets twice monthly from spring up to a month before the average first frost date for your area.

Lotus growing in the frost belt in winter must be placed at a depth beyond reach of ice. If the pond freezes to the bottom, handle lotus as suggested in Chapter 5 for hardy water lilies.

Harvesting and Planting Lotus Seeds

The hard protective covering on lotus seeds keep the life inside safe for centuries — seeds 500 years old have been successfully grown at Kenilworth Aquatic Gardens in Washington, D.C. It is rare for water gardeners to grow lotus from seed — tubers are preferred — but it can be done. When the seedpod has matured and is making its U-turn dive for the water, cut it off the plant. With your fingers, break the pod apart over a bowl. Store the seeds, which are about ½ inch long, in a sealed jar without water in a cool place until spring.

Plant lotus seeds about the same time you set out the parent tuber. With a wood or a metal file, file a notch in the seed covering to expose a bit of the white part. Set the seeds in a bowl with an inch or so of water over them and keep the bowl in a sunny window. In a week or two they will sprout. Fill a 4- or 5-inch pan with heavy garden soil, set the sprouted seeds on top, sprout side up, and press them gently into the soil. Cover the soil with rinsed gravel, and place the pan in the sun in the pond with 1 or 2 inches of water over the soil. Let the seedlings develop for several weeks, remove the weakest seedlings, and move the remaining few to a larger pan and a permanent place in the pond.

Dividing Lotus

The runners of lotus growing in a container divide and redivide each season and eventually bind the plant. In the frost belt a slowing of flower production five or six years after planting will signal that it is time to divide and repot. In frost-free areas you will need to divide sooner. The process is easy but exacting, and yields more lotus than you need or can ever give away. For the typical gardener, it is really a thinning process rather than propagation.

Lotus tubers must be harvested and divided early in the season before runners develop. When the first leaves are partway to the surface of the pond, with your fingers follow the stem down to the growing tip. Gently push into the soil under the growing tip and follow the tuber horizontally until you have passed two or, better, three joints. A joint is a node in the tuber from which little rootlets come out. You need at least two joints plus the growing tip for a successful transplant. Break the tuber off beyond the second or third joint and very carefully bring it to the surface. Discard any tubers that break. Plant each division as directed for planting tubers earlier in the chapter.

Another way to do this is to lift the container and, with a garden hose, gently spray out the soil around the tuber. Then use a sharp knife to cut the tuber off beyond the second or third joint from the growing tip. Excess tubers not used for planting can be sliced, fried in deep fat, and eaten!

9 ❧ Framing the Water Garden

YOU ARE MOST AWARE of the upright plants growing at the margins of the water when you approach the pond in the subdued light of early morning or at dusk. From the perspective of the house the vertical plants should rise on the far side or back of the pond, marking its boundaries, merging it with the garden, the lawn, the spider's web in the crook of a branch, the birds flying up to the trees — leading the eye from flat water to land plants and vaulting sky. Nature doesn't shift abruptly from floating lily pads to roses but instead uses plants that grow in the shallow water at the margins of the pond to make a gentle transition.

Narrow- and broad-leaved marginal plants are grown in containers set on the pond shelf or raised on upended pots, clean bricks, or weathered cinderblocks. Most succeed with 2 to 12 inches of water over the crown. These plants are of some help in removing nutrients that otherwise feed unwanted algae, but their main purpose is to frame the pond. Many are selected varieties of native plants that evolved in shallow water — bog plants, we call them. In a water garden the roots of these

Marginal plants frame a glassy pond where lilies bloom. Tall cattails are fronted by umbrella palm with yellow floating-heart and parrot's-feather at its feet. Upcurved lily pads, as at left, are often a sign that the plants are a little crowded. (Photo by Donald A. Ferguson)

173

exuberant growers are restricted by their soil containers. Because they grow straight up, the size of the container defines the space that irises and other narrow-leaved verticals will occupy at the surface. Be conservative in the number of irises and other narrow verticals you choose. You also need space along the margin of the pond for some of the broad-leaved plants described later in the chapter. These provide the bold splashes and substantial forms that add character to the pond design.

The Best Pond Irises

The showery March wind that turns the surface of the pond to gray crepe is the wake-up call for irises. Down in their soil containers young iris tips are thrusting up through the chilly muck seeking light, air, space. On the edges of swamps and wetlands new iris growth emerges early and displays the first brilliant flowers of the year in the solid green wall of bog plants. So it's natural when you are planning a home water garden to give these tall, grassy beauties the first choice of space on the pond shelf, if there is one, or on the floor of the pond raised on blocks or bricks.

Like the narrow- and broad-leaved marginal plants described below, irises provide the water garden with a crisp vertical contrast to the horizontals of the floating plants. Grass-green iris leaves grow tall in a matter of weeks. Close behind the leaves come stately flowering stems topped by multiple blooms cocooned in green. When they open in mid to late spring, the blossoms will show three uprising standards and three horizontal or down-turning falls — no beard. The French fleur-de-lys emblem was not inspired by a lily, by the way, but by one of these boggy irises. The colors of modern cultivated varieties and hybrids span the rainbow from white

Irises growing at the margins of the water garden at the Montreal Botanic Garden. (Photo by Elvin McDonald)

to yellow, pink, melon, brick red, and through the blues to violet and midnight purple. The only colors missing are fire-engine red, orange and green. All the irises have attractive foliage that remains long after flowering, a satisfying linear contrast to the pond's many horizontal planes.

Not all irises open early — there are late-season flowers, too. If space permits, you can have irises blooming from midspring to midsummer. The first to flower is the yellow flag, *Iris pseudacorus,* which is a bit larger than the others: in the deep South it develops a magnificent clump up to 5 feet tall.

The next color comes from the bright and beautiful Louisiana irises, then the regal Siberians take over. Japanese irises, whose exquisite blossoms can be 8 to 10 inches across, extend the season to midsummer, and in fall and winter their graceful, grassy leaves turn wonderful shades of russet and gold. Some Louisiana irises have leaves that are sword-shaped rather than grassy.

The pond irises are presented here in the order in which they usually bloom, from midspring to midsummer. Plant three rhizomes of each type in a container at least 5 inches across — one iris here and one there doesn't really work visually. Place the containers in the pond in full or partial sun, with 2 to 10 inches of water over the growing tips, or at the depths suggested below for individual plants.

Iris pseudacorus
Yellow flag

Hardiness varies with the variety

The yellow flag is a truly spectacular European iris that has naturalized along edges of ponds and quiet streams all over temperate North America. It forms handsome 3- to 5-foot-high clumps of 1- to 2-inch-wide parrot-green leaves. The vivid yellow flowers have brown or violet veins. They bloom in midspring in Zone 8, early summer in Zone 4. Hybrids range in color from white to dark yellow and grow about 4 feet high. There is a smaller, very desirable variegated hybrid about 2 feet tall. The beautiful double-flowered variety 'Flora Plena' is about the same height.

Culture: Easy to grow. Plant the rhizomes in containers in spring. The species grows well in full or half sun with up to 10 inches of water over the rhizomes. Set the double-flowered variety in full sun with only 4 inches over the crowns. The

Closeup of yellow flag, Iris pseudacorus. *(Photo by Bill Heritage)*

species is hardy in Zones 4 to 9; the doubles are hardy only in Zones 5 through 9.

Louisiana irises

Hardiness varies with the variety

The Louisiana irises, which flower from late spring into early summer, range in height from small, which means 18 to 24 inches tall, up to 5 feet. Three interesting wild American species native to warm boggy areas gave rise to the Louisiana cultivars and hybrids: *Iris fulva,* which has dainty flowers in coppery or reddish orange to salmon pink; *Iris foliosa,* which has white or bluish purple flowers and a zigzag stem; and *Iris giganticaerulea,* which flowers in every shade of lavender-blue. All have been hybridized, with the result that we now have irises in almost every color that thrive in water and in warm climates.

Culture: Place the container so that the growing tips have up to 6 inches of water over the soil. Individual Louisianas vary in hardiness, but most winter over in Zones 6 or 7 to 9. In

Iris fulva, *red iris, a wild American iris, grows well in shallow water or in very moist soil.*

The Louisiana iris 'Her Highness'.

Zones 6 and 7 fertilize in September and February; in Zones 8 and 9 fertilize in October and January.

'Dixie Deb'
ZONES 7–9

This is one of the first Louisianas to flower. It bears masses of sulfur-yellow blooms on a plant that may get up to 36 inches.

'Her Highness'
ZONES 7–9

From early to late spring, this regal plant produces very beautiful white flowers on stems up to 3 feet tall. The large, ruffled blossom has yellow-streaked signals and is truly eye-catching against its background of fresh green leaves.

'Marie Caillet'
ZONES 7–9

The large flowers are orchid-purple with a flash of yellow. They open in mid to late spring on plants up to 3 feet tall.

'Clyde Redmond'
ZONES 4–9

A favorite that blooms in midspring, the flower is a wonderful deep blue. The plant grows up to 2 feet tall and has narrow, graceful foliage.

'Black Gamecock'
ZONES 6–9

The flower of this spring bloomer is a rich blue-black with a brilliant streak of yellow-orange on the falls. The plant grows up to 2 feet tall. This particular cultivar does best with no more than 4 inches of water over the gravel.

Louisiana 'Clyde Redmond'.

'Eolian'
ZONES 7–9

In mid to late spring, big, showy flowers appear, a gorgeous sky blue with a flash of orange-yellow on the falls. This stately iris grows up to 24 inches tall.

'Bryce Leigh'
ZONES 7–9

This award-winning beauty is the Louisiana to plant for late blooms — early to midsummer. It displays two shades of pale lavender and has small yellow signals. The plant grows up to 30 inches tall.

Iris sibirica
Siberian iris
ZONES 4–9

The Siberians are among the most important garden flowers for color in mid to late spring and early summer. They thrive with up to 2 inches of water over the soil and play a star-

Siberian iris.

ring role in the water garden. The upright standards are small and don't quite meet above the exquisite large falls in showy colors — royal purple, lavender, white, maroon, pink, or yellow. There are two or three blossoms to a cluster, and they are good cutting flowers. The plant grows up to 2 or 3 feet tall, and the attractive grasslike foliage is handsome in every season.

Culture: Siberians bloom in soil that has a range of pH 5.0 to 8.0, but prefer moderately acid soils. Place the container where there will be 2 inches of water over the gravel. Successful in cold wet climates, the Siberians bloom in full or partial sun in the North; in the South, they do well in the sun but tolerate light shade or late afternoon shade.

I. versicolor
Blue flag
ZONES 4–9

This is the native American species that blooms in May and June in the wetlands of the eastern United States and Canada. The flowers are purplish or lavender-blue, the falls often veined and blotched. It is a good cutting flower, with three to five blooms on branched stems 2 to 3 feet tall. Farther south, a similar wild iris flourishes in water gardens — the swamp flag, *Iris virginica*. It opens a little earlier than the blue flag and grows to 24 inches tall. The flowers are soft blue or violet-blue, often streaked with yellow, green, and white. Narrow, graceful foliage makes it a perfect late iris.

Culture: Blue flag thrives in containers in a pond with up to 6 inches of water over the gravel.

I. ensata (synonym *kaempferi*)
Japanese iris
ZONES 4–8

Form and beauty have earned for these swamp flowers the nickname of orchid iris. They extend the iris season, blooming from late spring into early August on plants 2 to 3 feet tall. Each slender flowering stem bears two very large blue, pink, purple, mauve, or white blossoms. The flower crop is abundant, and some varieties will even bloom the first season from rhizomes set out that spring. The leaves are grasslike and turn wonderful shades of rust and gold in fall and winter. The clumps multiply and need division every three to five years.

Culture: The Japanese irises thrive in rich soil that is on the acid side, pH 5.5 to 6.5. Never, ever use lime! Set them in the pond in full or partial sun with up to 4 inches of water over the growing tips. In very hot climates, shade at noon will help to keep the foliage fresh and green. They prefer to be on the dry side in winter, so lift the containers and store them as directed for hardy water lilies. Japanese iris rhizomes winter very well buried in slightly damp peat moss in a place where the temperature is not below 40 degrees.

Iris Planting, Culture, Winter Care, and Division

The general instructions for planting and containers described in Chapter 5 apply to irises with a few differences. Iris rhizomes can be planted in spring, summer, or early fall. If started in early autumn, they typically bloom the following year; if planted in early spring they — except sometimes for the Japanese irises — probably won't flower until the next spring. The planting procedures are the same in all three seasons. Plant one to three iris rhizomes in a soil container about 9 inches across that has been filled with heavy, slightly acid garden soil, pH 5.5 to 6.5.

Plant the rhizomes at a slant so that the bottom is under 2 inches of soil and the growing tip just above the soil. As the irises go out of bloom, remove the dead flowers and eventually the flowering stems. Fertilize lightly every year in fall and early spring. Hardy irises winter successfully in their containers if they are cut back and lowered beyond the reach of ice. Lift containerized irises that are not hardy in your area and provide winter care as suggested for the hardy water lilies.

In Zones 7 and northward iris rhizomes benefit from being divided every three to five years. In Zones 8 and 9 they need dividing every year or two. They can be divided most successfully after they have finished blooming, in mid to late summer or in early fall. Following procedures similar to those recommended for a water lily, cut the rhizome apart, providing 2 or more inches of rhizome for each growing tip. Replant each growing tip just as you planted the parent. Discard the old rhizome.

The Best Narrow-leaved Verticals

The marginal plants that have very narrow leaves give the water garden the vertical motion and sound of tall grasses. With even a slight breeze, the plants sway and rustle. A gorgeous few, like the spider lily, follow the irises into bloom. Others are chosen for the contrast created by their linear form and for their varied textures and foliage colors. Reedy plants like the cattails bring something to every season. The rustling sounds of summer are followed in fall by the tick-tock movement of the round brown cattails straight and stiff as pokers. When winter comes, the cattails maintain the pond's vertical dimension. If the water garden is well sited, from the house on a frosty morning you will see them standing like golden sentinels in the snow.

One group (two or three of a kind) of narrow-leaved plants — variegated iris, small cattail, or a low clump of equisetum — is enough for a tub or kettle garden. A pond 4 to 5 feet across has space for one clump of iris and one of variegated sweet flag, *Acorus calamus* — a beautiful plant. In a pond 10 to 15 feet across, in addition to these two you might include three dwarf bamboo and three leafier plants such as sagittaria, which bears pretty little white flowers.

There are both frost-hardy and frost-tender perennials among the marginal aquatics, and a few grow from rhizomes. Most can be transplanted readily from spring through summer. These plants are presented in alphabetical order.

Variegated Acorus calamus, *sweet flag, is a lovely 2-foot variety of this fragrant marginal plant.*

Acorus calamus

Sweet flag, calamus

ZONES 4–11

A medium-size, grassy, semi-evergreen perennial 30- to 36-inches tall, sweet flag is handsome even in small ponds. In summer it puts up flowering stalks that bear small brown-green catkins. When crushed, the irislike leaves give off a sweet, lemony scent; *Acorus* was one of the strewing herbs spread on the floors of ancient castles to mask unpleasant odors, and for centuries the leaves have been used to make baskets and wreaths. Calamus root, dried and ground, becomes a scented powder that is used to anchor the fragrant oils in potpourris and pomanders. The leaves of a lovely but less fragrant 2-foot-tall variegated species, *A. c.* 'Variegatus', are edged with bold cream stripes and flushed with rose in spring.

Culture: Plant with up to 6 inches of water over the crown. Sweet flag thrives in full or partial sun, and though it tolerates some shade it grows more slowly there.

Butomus umbellatus
Flowering rush
Zones 3–7

All summer long, this low-growing grassy perennial produces delicate, slightly fragrant, very attractive rose-pink flowers. Phloxlike individual florets stretch out on elegant, spidery 5-inch stems. The narrow leaves have a triangular cross-section and are 20 to 30 inches long. A native of Europe, flowering rush is outstanding in the cool, wet Pacific Northwest but fares poorly where temperatures consistently reach 90 degrees or higher.

Culture: Plant root divisions and set them in the pond with up to 6 inches of water over the crown, in sun or partial sun.

Cotula coronopifolia
Brass-buttons
Zones 8–9

Sometimes offered under the name golden buttons, this little plant is 6 to 12 inches tall and has narrow, spear-shaped leaves. In summer it bears small, bright yellow flowers. It is outstanding in cool, wet climates like those of the Pacific Northwest and Britain.

Culture: Plant with the crowns in 1 or 2 inches of water and in full sun. It may winter over on the West Coast in Zones 7–9.

Dulichium arundinaceum
Dwarf bamboo
Zones 6–11

This low-growing, feathery, bamboolike plant stays under 15 to 18 inches tall and is not overly invasive. The slender leaf

Spike rush, Eleocharis, *is an ideal linear plant for a small pond.*

blades come away from the main stem in an especially attractive way. Insignificant catkins appear in summer. Dwarf bamboo is good for low screening in the pond and is a choice accent plant for a tub garden. Though it is very desirable, only a few nurseries carry it.

Culture: Plant root divisions in spring or summer and set the container in the pond with up to 4 inches of water over the crown. In areas colder than Zone 6 it is grown as an annual. Full or partial sun.

Eleocharis
Spike rush
Hardiness varies with the species

This genus has quill-shaped leaves tipped in summer and fall by curious but attractive little light brown seed heads. For water gardens, the two species described below are the best choices.

Culture: Plant the rhizomes in containers in spring or summer and grow them in full or partial sun.

E. montevidensis
Spike rush
Zones 6–9

This rushlike plant up to 12 inches tall is excellent for small water gardens and is especially attractive edging a corner of a pond. It has the dainty, narrow, quill-shaped leaves and light brown seed heads typical of the genus. Plant it with 2 inches of water over the crown.

E. tuberosa
Chinese water chestnut
Zones 7–11

Up to 3 feet tall, this is a larger spike rush and the better choice for larger ponds. It grows from a compact tuber or corm that in the Orient is used as a food. Plant it with up to 12 inches of water over the crown.

Equisetum hyemale, *horsetail, a jointed, reedlike accent plant.*

Equisetum hyemale
Horsetail
Zones 3–11

This low-growing, trim, linear evergreen plant makes dense stands of slim, dark green jointed stems about a foot high that come straight up from the rootstock. There are neither leaves nor flowers, but spikelike spore-bearing cones appear in summer and fall. It looks just right in a water garden, probably because we are so accustomed to seeing it growing wild in or near wet places.

Culture: Plant root divisions any time from spring to fall and place the container in the pond with up to 6 inches of water over the crown. Horsetail prefers shade in warm regions but tolerates full sun in a cool climate.

Hymenocallis liriosme
Spider lily
Zones 8–11

The plant has attractive foliage, but it is grown for its flower — a large, white blossom that is sweetly scented and elegant. From late spring to midsummer, the flowering stalks, each bearing up to six blooms, rise from the bulb. They open one at a time and last for two or three days: as one finishes, another opens. In Zones 8 and 9 in the deep South the plant grows to 4 feet tall, but only to 3 feet in cooler climates. The 2-foot-tall variegated spider lily, *H. caribaea* var. *variegata*, has boldly striped foliage and the same beautiful white flowers. This is a striking accent plant but more difficult to grow than the species. Planted together they make a glorious show.

Culture: These frost-tender bulbs are perennial only in warm regions. In cooler regions where daytime temperatures

The exquisite blossoms of Hymenocallis liriosme, *spider lily.*

regularly rise above 75 degrees, they are grown as annuals and discarded at the end of the season. Plant in midspring and set the container with up to 6 inches of water over the bulb. Full or partial sun.

Mimulus luteus
Monkey flower

Hardiness uncertain

A lovely, low-growing flowering marginal, 1 to 2 feet high, it bears brilliant yellow blossoms that look something like a snapdragon and a pansy and have dark red or purple spots and splotches. The plant blooms over a long period from summer to autumn and often reblooms if it is cut back after flowering. The species has given rise to some strikingly marked large-flowered varieties. A great plant for water gardens in regions with climates like that of the Pacific Northwest, it prefers shaded situations and is especially attractive growing near ferns.

Culture: Plant with up to 1 or 2 inches of water over the crown, in partial sun or shade. At this writing, its hardiness is not certain.

Sagittaria lancifolia **form** *ruminoides*
Red-stemmed sagittaria

Zones 7–11

The leaves of this medium-size species are perhaps ¼ inch wider than grass, and flare out to 2 and 3 inches wide from bold red stems that are about 4 feet tall at maturity. In summer sprays of pretty white flowers appear; each blossom has a green center. Some first-rate sagittarias with broad leaves shaped like arrowheads are listed among the broad-leaved marginals later in the chapter.

Culture: These semitender bulbs are perennial only in warm regions. In cooler regions where daytime temperatures regularly rise above 75 degrees, they are grown as annuals and discarded at the end of the season. Plant in spring, summer, or fall, in full sun with up to 6 or 7 inches of water over the crowns. Division is most successful in spring or summer.

Scirpus tabernaemontani 'Albescens'
White bulrush
ZONES 5–11

An upright grassy plant with cylindrical leaves that are nearly white with vertical green stripes. The leaves are 4 to 6 feet tall. In summer it bears insignificant white flowers. Use this as a white accent in the water garden.

Culture: Plant in spring or summer and set the container in the pond with up to 6 inches of water over the crown. Full or partial sun.

Typha
Cattail
Hardiness varies with the variety

Some version of this towering reedlike clump, which reaches 6 or 8 feet, grows in just about every wet place on our continent. The long, narrow, stiff leaves are borne on unbranched stems. In late summer spikes of beige florets top slender stalks, and in early fall these become the velvety brown seed heads we call cattails. They persist through winter, making this a superb screening plant. For the water garden there are several handsome types, all similar but with interesting and useful differences.

Culture: Plant in spring, summer, or fall (at least a month before killing frost), and set the container in the pond

Typha, *cattail*.

with up to 12 inches of water over the crown. Grows in full or partial sun. Hardiness varies with each species and variety.

T. angustifolia
Narrow-leaved cattail
ZONES 2–11

A nice tall plant, about 7 feet, with narrow leaves that catch every wind. The cattails are an attractive light brown. A graceful plant to use for screening.

T. latifolia
Cattail
ZONES 2–11

This is the common cattail that grows in the wild in dense stands almost 8 feet tall. In a water garden it makes a striking accent plant. The variegated *T. l.* var. *variegata* is more beautiful and grows half as tall. Though more difficult to transplant, it is definitely worth a try.

T. laxmannii
Graceful cattail
ZONES 3–11

This medium-size cattail is just right for a tub garden or a small pond. In a big water garden, it is very attractive growing at the side of the larger *T. latifolia*. The leaves are narrow, and the overall height at maturity is about 4 feet. The seed heads mature somewhat earlier than in larger species.

Ornamental Grasses

Even in the still heat of summer, the restless ornamental grasses manage to dance and whisper. One or two species growing in or out of the water enhance a pond site. They are especially lovely in their fall colors of gold and honey. The following varieties grow with 1 to 2 inches of water over their roots and are available from most garden centers.

Calamagrostis acutiflora 'Stricta', feather reed grass, is 5 to 7 feet tall and bears fluffy bluish flower panicles that in fall turn golden tan and catch the light; *Chasmanthium latifolium*, northern oats, 3 to 5 feet tall with arching leaves, is spangled with fruit heads in summer and turns bronze in fall; *Glyceria aquatica* 'Vanelson' is a mounded grass with lovely cream- and green-striped leaves, 18 to 30 inches tall, that take on a rosy tint in early spring and fall; *Miscanthus sinensis* 'Gracillimus', maiden grass, is a beautiful 5- to 6-foot grass with gorgeous fall and winter colors. It is a favorite for drying and as a subject of Japanese brush paintings; *Panicum virgatum,* switch-grass, which grows upright 3 to 7 feet tall, is covered with clouds of deep red to purple spikelets in summer and turns bright yellow in fall; *Pennisetum alopecuroides,* rose fountain grass, a fine-leaved arching grass that reaches 3 feet all around at maturity.

The Best Broad-leaved Verticals

The narrow-leaved vertical plants bring to the margins of the water garden the fluid grace and movement you see in fields of grain. The bold uprights of the broad-leaved marginals add substance at heights ranging from 1 to 14 feet. In a breeze, the immense elephant's-ear leaves of colocasia and the thalias flap and woggle on their stems, and the umbrella palms dance. The broad-leaved marginals take some nutrients from the water and provide the pond with some shade, but their real contribution is contrast in form. The biggest broad-leaved verticals stand out almost like statues, broadcasting advances in the season.

When the first strong flush of green rises in the broad-leaved marginals, you look for action in the goldfish. Summer announces lotus time by fluffing out the red and gold cannas and scenting the garden with the bog lily's pure white blossoms. Autumn is heralded by a fading of the green in the big leaves, and when they begin to yellow you know frost has stopped by. After the first few freezes some pond owners cut all the verticals down to clear the water at once of decaying vegetation. It's a healthy practice. Others prefer to leave some of these beautiful dried arrangements through fall and early winter, and that's all right, too. Enjoy the plants as long as they remain standing. Eventually, one by one, they collapse as frost breaks them down. When you see this happening, promptly cut them back to their crowns.

Unlikely as it seems, most broad-leaved marginals don't take up much more surface space than the narrow-leaved upright plants. As with the narrow-leaved marginals, the container size tends to define the surface area the plants will occupy, for most arrange their leaves according to the headroom available. As the foliage rises above the surface it does spread out a foot or so beyond the perimeter of the soil container, but even then most broad-leaved plants clump rather tidily. There are exceptions, such as the handsome, sprawling water arum and *Thalia dealbata,* which is something of a space eater. Appropriate containers are tubs or pails 7 or more inches across for each set of three plants. Place them 1 or 2 feet apart on the pond shelf or on raised platforms on the pond floor.

A tub or kettle garden that is home to one miniature water lily can accommodate just one hardy or one tropical broad-leaved marginal plant, perhaps a hardy water pickerel rush or a tropical umbrella palm. Without a lily, a tub can handle three or four marginals. A lily pond 4 or 5 feet across has space for six hardy or six tropical or tender perennial marginals. You might choose three pickerel rushes and three lizard's-tails or three umbrella palms and three dwarf papyrus. In a pond 10 to 15 feet across, you can plant nine hardy or nine tropical marginals. For instance, three each of pickerel rush, lizard's-tail, and thalia or three each of umbrella palm, dwarf papyrus, and Longwood canna. In a large lily pond massing eight to twelve identical plants — canna or pickerel rush or thalia, for example — in a tub 16 by 24 inches has great impact.

There are herbaceous perennials among the broad-leaved marginals, and a few grow from rhizomes. These plants are presented in alphabetical order.

Alisma plantago-aquatica
Water plantain
ZONES 5–8

A low-growing cormous perennial, alisma holds its handsome pointed oval green leaves about 6 inches above the surface. In summer it sends airy panicles of tiny white florets soaring up 3 feet. In full bloom, it reminds you of baby's-breath. This is an outstanding plant in climates like that of the Pacific Northwest, but it wilts away in regions where summers are hot.

Culture: Plant in full sun with up to 10 inches of water over the crown.

Canna × *hybrida*
Canna
ZONES 7–11

The canna hybrids resemble land cannas in flower and plant form: they grow 4 to 6 feet tall and bloom in brilliant reds and golds. A very satisfying sequence is yellow flag, *Iris pseudacorus,* with its sunny flowers in midspring, followed by the cannas' brilliant midsummer blooms. The hybrids developed by Longwood Gardens (Kennett Square, Pennsylvania) have many more blossoms than the species and include salmon among their colors. The variegated canna, *C. americanallis* var. *variegata,* has clear orange flowers and leaves with showy cream-colored stripes.

Culture: In Zones 7 through 10, plant this tender perennial in spring or summer; in Zone 11, set cannas out any time. In Zones 3 through 6, where summer temperatures go above

The beautiful hybrid Longwood water canna, Canna × hybrida.

75 degrees, canna is grown as an annual; it can be lifted in fall, stored, and returned to the pond in spring. Canna grows best in full sun with up to 6 inches of water over the crown.

Colocasia
Elephant's-ear
Zones 9–11
Colocasias are frost-tender perennials that produce huge, heavily veined leaves shaped like an arrowhead or elephant's ear.

The leaf is held at a sharp angle at the top of its stalk, and in size and coloring, colocasias seem tropical and exotic. In summer small pale yellow flowers like calla lilies bloom down among the leaves on short stems.

Culture: In Zones 3 through 8 where summer temperatures rise above 75 degrees, colocasia is grown as an annual; it is lifted in fall, stored, and returned to the pond in spring. The species here succeed in any light. They grow well in damp soil. They lose vigor as the water depth increases.

C. affinis var. *Jenningsii*
Black princess taro

This bold, shade-loving variety has dark green leaves overlaid with black and grows to about 42 inches high. Plant with up to 6 inches of water over the crown.

C. esculenta
Taro

Also known as dasheen, the plant grows to about 3½ feet tall and has 2-foot-long velvety green leaves that often display brilliant white veins. In Hawaii and the South Sea islands the root is pounded and cooked to make a starchy staple called poi. (Without proper preparation it is toxic.) The species grows with up to 12 inches of water over the crown. 'Hilo Beauty' is a beautiful, slightly smaller cultivar with green leaves mottled in ivory; transplant it with not more than 2 inches of water over the crown.

C. e. var. *fontanesii*
Violet-stemmed taro

The violet stems of this big, gorgeous variety put the plant in a class by itself. In warm regions, it grows to 42 inches tall.

Crinum americanum
Bog lily
Zones 8–11

This small bulb bears one of summer's most beautiful flowers. The funnel-shaped, pure white, lily-scented blossoms have greenish throats and rise in clusters above 2-foot tufts of curving, straplike leaves. Each stalk produces only a few flowers, and the first season there won't be many, but each flower is very worthwhile. In subsequent years multiple clumps develop, and you will get a larger crop of blossoms.

Culture: Crinum is a tender bulb that is grown as a perennial only in warm regions. In cooler areas it is lifted in fall and stored in its container for winter, as described for hardy water lilies. Set the bulbs out in spring with up to 6 inches of water over the growing tip. Crinum prefers full sun but tolerates partial shade.

Cyperus
Cyperus
Zones 9–11

Several species of this tropical evergreen, including papyrus, the big plant from which the early Egyptians made paper, are popular. Cyperus foliage grows at the top of a reedy stalk; the narrow, grassy leaves that radiate outward like the ribs of an airy umbrella flow and dance in the wind. The flower is green, then yellow or brown, and is likely to interest only botanists. Late in the season the mature stalks bend down and enter the water, and grow new plants that develop viviparously from the center of the umbrella. In its natural state, when the parent branch dies, young plants drift over the water looking for soil in which to root and begin life. Though it must be reset outdoors every spring in cool regions, cyperus is so interesting and decorative that most gardeners make the effort.

Culture: In Zones 3 through 8 where summer temperatures exceed 75 degrees, plant cyperus in spring or summer. You can easily winter the plant indoors in a sunny room. Be sure that its soil is damp or covered by an inch or so of water. You can propagate for the next year's planting by cutting off and rooting plantlets and wintering them indoors in a sunny window with 1 to 2 inches of water over the gravel. In warm regions, plant cyperus any time and treat it as a perennial. Place the container in the pond in full or partial sun or in shade, with up to 6 inches of water over the crown.

C. alternifolius
Umbrella palm

Big, though not the biggest papyrus grown, the 5-foot-tall umbrella palm provides good screening, and in a large pond it makes a handsome accent plant.

C. haspan
Dwarf papyrus

This plant produces dainty tufts of foliage at the top of a stem that grows up to 30 inches tall; it is just right for tubs and small water gardens. The tops of mature stalks send out spindlelike green rays tipped by green seedpods that turn brown. An attractive and successful houseplant, it is grown with 1 to 2 inches of water over the crown.

C. papyrus
Egyptian paper reed

Used in ancient Egypt as a raw material for paper and woven baskets, this is a stately reed with a bold presence. In tropical

The graceful foliage of the umbrella palm, Cyperus alternifolius.

Ferns, the dainty tassels of dwarf papyrus, and a stand of spike rush frame a small water garden. (Photo by Elvin McDonald)

and semitropical climates, it grows to 14 feet: in cooler regions it reaches 8 or 10 feet before the cold breaks it down. There is a theory that Moses was hidden among tall papyrus reeds in a basket made of papyrus, not bulrushes, as stated by the English translators of the King James Bible, more familiar perhaps with English bulrushes than with Egyptian flora.

Eichhornia paniculata
Brazilian pickerel rush
ZONES 8–11
This Brazilian relative of water hyacinth is a frost-tender perennial (it can be grown from seed every year) bog plant with pale

violet-blue flowers. It grows 20 to 30 inches high and comes under the same legal restrictions as water hyacinth.

Culture: Plant in a soil container covered with gravel and set in the pond in full sun with 1 to 5 inches of water over the gravel.

Houttuynia cordata var. *variegata*
Chameleon plant
ZONES 6–11

This lovely, low, spreading perennial aquatic grows 12 to 24 inches high and is valued for its aromatic, multicolored leaves. The broad, heart-shaped, leathery leaves are edged in green and streaked with yellowish white and red shading to maroon. In spring a few small white flowers appear.

Culture: Houttoynia succeeds as an annual in Zones 3 through 5 where summer temperatures rise above 75 degrees. Sun enhances the coloring, but the plant also thrives in some shade. Plant with up to 4 inches of water over the crown.

Mentha aquatica
Water mint
ZONES 6–11

This very pungent herb loves water. The brisk scent of the crushed leaves was a favorite for chasing stale household odors, and it has been bred into one of today's most widely used herbs, peppermint, *M.* × *piperita.* If you prefer mint with a hint of lemon, plant *M.* × *p.* var. *citrata,* which also thrives with wet feet. Water mint multiplies extravagantly, creating an aromatic blue-green jungle 6 inches high, a charming softener when it is trained to grow along the edges of the pond. In the eastern United States water mint has escaped cultivation, and in wild watery places in midsummer you will occasionally come across its purple flower spikes lifted in a mass of crinkly bright green mint leaves.

Culture: Plant in early spring or summer, and set in the pond with up to 4 inches of water over the crown. Thrives in sun, partial sun, or light shade.

Orontium aquaticum
Golden-club
ZONES 6–11

A low-growing native of wet places, golden-club is found in the wild in the eastern part of North America. Dark green velvety oval leaves, 6 to 8 inches long, are nicely arranged on or just a little above the water. From spring to early summer the plant sends up 10- to 12-inch-high, pencil-slim, slightly curving, white flowering spikes tipped with very small golden yellow blossoms. The flowers are followed by blue-green berries.

Culture: Plant with 1 to 6 inches of water over the crown in partial sun or filtered light. Plant any time in Zone 11 in spring or summer in cooler regions.

Peltandra virginica
Water arum
ZONES 5–9

Of medium size but big-leaved and bold, this native of eastern North America is a hardy, handsome, carefree addition to the water garden. Glossy leaves shaped like arrowheads, up to 1 foot long, develop on stately stems 2 or 3 feet tall. Like the jack-in-the-pulpit, it produces a spathe, which many viewers refer to as a flower. The flowers are tiny and yellow. Allow surface space for the foliage, which spreads up to 3 feet.

A white-flowered variety of pickerel rush, Pontederia cordata, blooms with a hardy white water lily. (Photo by Ronnie and Jeannie Luttrell)

Culture: Plant in spring or summer in full or partial sun with up to 6 inches of water over the crown.

Pontederia cordata
Pickerel rush
ZONES 3–11

This native American wildflower, one of the best all-around medium-size marginal plants, makes lovely bouquets. From spring through summer clumps of waxy leaves 2 to 3 feet tall are topped by spikes densely covered with blue flowers. Typically, each blossom has two yellow dots on the upper petal. A white-flowered form thrives only in full sun.

Culture: Plant any time from early spring to a month before the first expected frost, with 1 to 12 inches of water over the crown. The species succeeds in full or partial sun or some shade.

Sagittaria
Arrowhead
Hardiness varies with the variety

The sagittaria species recommended here have much broader leaves than those listed with the narrow-leaved plants. They are counted among the most decorative of the medium-size marginals. The leaves are shaped like arrowheads, and in summer the flowering stems bear clusters of attractive, three-petaled white flowers, each with the yellow dot that is characteristic of this plant.

Culture: Plant bulbs in spring in full sun at the depths described for each species. Or transplant between spring and a month prior to killing frost. The roots can be successfully divided in summer.

Double-flowered arrowhead,
Sagittaria sagittifolia
'Flore Pleno'.

S. latifolia
Arrowhead
ZONES 4–11

Duck potato is another common name for arrowhead; the starchy root is eaten by Native Americans. A hardy plant about 24 inches tall, it bears clusters of the white flowers typical of the sagittarias. Plant in full or partial sun with up to 6 inches of water over the crown.

S. montevidensis
Giant arrowhead
ZONES 4–11

Another 4-foot-tall arrowhead, this species flourishes in warm regions, reseeding itself from one season to the next. The flowers are white, often with a purple blotch at the base of each petal. Plant with up to 6 inches of water over the crown.

S. sagittifolia 'Flore Pleno'
Double old-world arrowhead
ZONES 6–11

A 4-foot-tall cultivar with showy, truly double white flowers, 'Flore Pleno' doesn't transplant easily, but once established it is very rewarding. It sometimes is offered as *Sagittaria japonica*. Plant with up to 7 inches of water over the crown.

Saururus cernuus
Lizard's-tail
ZONES 4–9

This native American perennial aquatic, about 24 inches high, sends amazingly long, slender, cream-colored flower spikes arching over its crowded foliage. The flowers appear in summer and are somewhat fragrant. Lizard's-tail is grown primarily for its aromatic, heart-shaped green leaves, but the unusual form of the flowers will fix the common name in your thoughts.

Culture: Plant in spring or summer in full or partial sun, with up to 6 inches of water over the crown.

Thalia

Thalia

Hardiness varies with the species

The big, strikingly handsome thalias described here are perennials native to the warmer regions of North America. Typically their pointed oval leaves are carried at a right angle to the rigid stems. In summer airy little violet to purple flowers soar above the leaves. These are superb accent plants for water gardens large and small.

Culture: Plant in spring or summer with 1 to 12 inches of water over the crown in full or partial sun.

T. dealbata

Zones 6–11

This big, fairly hardy thalia produces leaf stems 4 to 6 feet tall; the deep purple flowers rise 1 to 5 feet above the leaf tops. It is sometimes referred to as hardy canna. Plant it with up to 12 inches of water over the crown.

T. geniculata var. ruminoides

Red-stemmed thalia

Zones 9–11

This big, dramatic cold-tender perennial from Florida was introduced to the aquatic trade by San Diego aquatic specialist Walter Pagels; it is now the preferred variety of thalia. Its 5-foot red or purple foliage stems are topped by flowers that

Thalia dealbata *is called hardy canna for its purple flowers on long stems.*

can soar to 10 feet. The blossoms are more violet than those of hardy thalia. Set the plant out in spring or summer in full sunlight with up to 6 inches of water over the crown. It succeeds as an annual in Zones 5 through 8 where summer temperatures rise above 75 degrees.

Planting, Culture, Winter Care, and Division

The hardy marginal plants can be set out when the pond water exceeds about 49 degrees. But wait until the pond water temperature is above 69 degrees before setting out the annuals and tender perennials.

Set out individual plants in 5-inch-diameter pans or pails that hold at least 3½ quarts of soil. For groups of plants, provide round, oval, or square pans 24 inches across. Make one or two small holes in the bottoms of the containers to guarantee the plants access to water in case the pond level falls below the soil container rim. Partially fill the containers with slightly acid garden soil that includes a small amount of humus and fertilize lightly.

Marginals are most often arranged at the far end of the pond on a shelf or on submerged blocks. They look very good planted in groups of three of the same species. Don't combine different species in one group because a super-aggressive type will always crowd out the others. Start small young plants — 6 inches high or less — in the pond with an inch of water over the gravel in their containers. As they mature they can be moved to deeper water, as recommended for each variety.

From spring until a month before the first expected frost, fertilize the perennials monthly at the strength recommended on the fertilizer label. Throughout the growing season remove dead foliage and flowers. At the end of the season, any annuals should be pulled up and added to the garden compost pile. Tender perennials don't have a dormant season. In the frost belt they can't be stored for the winter like tender garden perennials — geraniums, for instance. They are most often treated as annuals and discarded when cold comes, but if you move them to a sunny greenhouse pond, they will continue there and even grow a little.

In frost-free climates the tender perennials are left in the pond, where their growth and flowering will slow until the coldest part of the winter is over. At that time, prune and groom them and prepare them for the growing season ahead with a monthly fertilization.

In cold regions the hardy perennials turn yellow when frosts come. Sometime between the first hard frost and the end of December, cut them back to within a few inches of their crowns. In a water garden that will ice over, it is best to cut back hardy marginals growing in pans and pails and lower them out of reach of the ice. But do *not* cut cattails below the water line — this can kill them. They look attractive in the pond throughout the winter. Handle containerized hardy perennials that aren't hardy in your zone as suggested for water lilies.

Divide perennial marginals as you would similar land plants. Use a shovel to quarter the great big ones; use a clean, sharp knife or your hands to cut or break apart smaller plants. Plant the best and share or discard the others.

10   Fish, Snails, and Other Small Helpers

Among the sinuous stems of the water lilies, golden pond fish weave enchanting serpentines — but that's not the whole of their appeal. Their response to human attention is so endearing that some owners caress them, and a few have even been known to kiss their fish. Many give them names. Goldfish will live ten to fifteen years, and koi will live for decades unless they meet up with a predator, disease, parasite, or disagreeable water quality. Fish are the easiest pets you'll ever know. They don't need to be housebroken or walked. They won't keep your neighbors up at night. If you go away for two or three weeks, a kennel isn't necessary, and Aunt Betty doesn't have to drive over to feed them. The pond might be clearer when you come back from a trip because the fish have had to find their own food. In a balanced pond the fish dine rather well on submerged plants such as elodea and *Cabomba,* on the mosslike algae on the pond sides, and on insects and larvae.

Fish and their scavenger associates perform functions that are essential to the water garden's health and ecological balance. Without them, in warm weather still water becomes an insect factory and polluted. The colorful goldfish, golden

A group of curious goldfish, speckled shubunkins, and Japanese fantails create an underwater mural.

209

orfe, and Japanese koi will, along with frogs, keep down the population of mosquitoes and other undesirable insects. Snails and tadpoles also help keep the water free of leftover fish food. The magic formula in Chapter 5 details the combination of plants, fish, and scavengers considered optimum for keeping a pond in balance. The thing most likely to upset the balance of a pond is too much affection for the fish.

The Fish

One of the few mistakes you can make with a water garden is to give in to the temptation to save all of the fish fry. In early spring you will be charmed by the courting ritual as three or four males chase a swollen female, eager to fertilize the spawn she deposits. If you haven't provided a spawning mat or net, the fish will deposit their eggs on the undulating fronds of the submerged plants. They hatch in three to seven days, backing tail first out of their birth bubbles, then wiggle free. The first day or so they stand vertically in the water, eyes twice as wide as the rest of the body. It takes them almost twenty-four hours to fill their swim bladders with the little bit of air that lets them assume a horizontal position and swim off to explore their world.

Left to nature, relatively few of the fry will survive — only as many as the pond's resources can support. But the fry will want to eat quite a bit, and you'll feel an almost irresistible desire to feed them. If you give in to that desire, you will be astonished at how many baby fish you can save in one season. There won't begin to be enough space for all those babies in the pond, and certainly no space for next year's crop. If you are going to save the fry, you must be prepared to build additional ponds or to spend a lot of time finding homes for your extra pets.

If all — or even most — of the fry are saved, that will initiate a natural sequence that begins with small fry being eaten by larger fish. The extra fish food you put into the pond for the fry, and the waste generated as the fish population builds, will load the pond with more nutrients than the submerged plants can absorb. Next comes algae bloom, signaled by a rich and growing green in the water. Algae need water, nutrients (like those generated by fish waste), warmth, and light to grow. Eventually they use up the available supplies and suddenly die, as do algae in natural ponds when things get out of balance.

In the process of decaying, organic matter can consume oxygen faster than the water can absorb it from the air. When fish lack oxygen, they die. The bigger fish die first. Smaller fish can tolerate water with a low oxygen content a little longer. This is nature's way of clearing away excess while giving the young their chance to reproduce. Excess algae bloom is a cause of fish kills in our rivers and lakes as well as in garden ponds.

Overcrowded fish trigger another of nature's population controls: their bright colors and increased activity attract fish-eating predators. Fish-eating birds, turtles, water snakes, and frogs all prey on fish, but the most feared predators in a home pond are raccoons. They're good fishermen, persistent, inventive, hungry, and much more trouble than cats. A cat attracted by a lot of tails swishing will take to sitting on the edge of the pond to watch the show. But the truth is, cats aren't very serious fish pond predators. A cat fishing in a fish bowl can cause devastation because it will make strike after strike until successful. In an outdoor pond the cat has one stroke, then opportunity vanishes as the fish flash to the bottom or the opposite side. The cat, meanwhile, is likely to be swimming, which is not its favorite sport.

Yet another way nature keeps fish populations in balance is through pathogens — parasites and diseases. The job of pathogens is to bring a system back into balance when population growth has gone too far. Pathogens are always present in pond water. You are likely to become aware of them only if the fish are stressed by crowding, poor water quality, handling, or fear. If the fish become listless, first check the pH of the water; too low (or high) a reading is not good for fish. If the pH isn't to blame, you'll find help at a local pet shop or water garden specialist. They deal routinely with other conditions that can cause listlessness: a high level of ammonia or nitrite from fish waste; toxic materials such as insecticides; or parasites and diseases.

Feeding Makes Friends

It's a fact that a few fish in a pond well stocked with appropriate plants don't need to be fed. However, fish that you don't feed will remain wild. They will hide when you come to the pond, vanishing with a swish of the tail into the submerged plants or under the lily pads. Feeding creates a relationship rather rapidly with goldfish and koi; golden orfe are less responsive.

Fish food generally comes in floating form as flakes, sticks, or pellets or in sinking granular form. Flake food serves both large and small fish. Even fish fry can eat it if you crumble it finely between your fingers. Pellets or sticks come in various sizes for goldfish and koi 2 or more inches long. Granular food, for fish over an inch long, is economical and has the advantage of not requiring the fish to expose themselves to potential predators at the surface.

Once the fish have been introduced to their new home (see "Releasing Fish and Other Small Helpers" in Chapter 5) and are swimming around in a leisurely fashion, settle down by the pond in a spot where you can relax. Slowly lean over the water and gently drop in a few fish flakes or pellets. Sudden movements will scare the fish. Don't concentrate the food where the fish are gathering. If you do, the smallest fish will be pushed away by the bigger fish. You'll know you are overfeeding if the fish let some of the floating food sink to the bottom of the pond — there it will nourish the algae that makes the water murky. Don't give more than the fish will eat in five minutes, or you could overload the pond with nutrients that stimulate algae growth, creating an excess the plants will not be able to absorb. Wait quietly for the fish to find the food. Don't worry if they fail to find it. Try again the next day.

If you continue feeding the fish regularly at about the same hour and place for two or three weeks, they will begin to come to the feeding spot when you arrive. They may even gather before you appear. Place a little more food in front of loners and nervous nellies. Feed in several places if some of the fish can't seem to get their share. In time the fish will become

Trained goldfish will gather at a particular spot at feeding time. Between hand-fed meals, they gobble insects and larvae. (Photo by Emerson Freese)

tame and will nudge your fingers. If you are patient they will even learn to eat from your hand and accept stroking.

Younger fish eat more than older fish and enjoy being fed several times a day. A maintenance diet for fish is 3 percent of their body weight a day. A growth diet is 5 percent. The percentage of body weight for young fish is higher because they are growing, but bigger fish on a maintenance diet may be eating much more than the young fish. If you want to feed your fish more but want your water to remain clear or nearly clear, add extra submerged plants or install a filter — preferably a biological filter — or use an algicide regularly.

In hot weather the metabolic rate of the fish — the rate at which they convert food to energy — speeds up and they eat more. They also eat more in fall to prepare for winter. However, as the water temperature drops to 50 degrees or so, their body processes slow down and they eat less. Stop feeding when the temperature reaches 45 degrees, for then they can no longer digest the food. In the frost belt they spend winter in the deepest part of the pond, dormant: if disturbed, they'll swim a bit but will go right back to their winter rest.

Goldfish

Four types of shining, brilliantly colored goldfish have become the enduring guardians of our water gardens — comets, Japanese fantails, shubunkins, and calico fantails. Goldfish, *Carassius auratus,* were imported into the United States from China in the nineteenth century. When a sport with an elongated tail was observed, it was bred and named the comet. These tough, streamlined fish and the exquisitely graceful double-tailed Japanese fantails are scaled fish that start out metallic silver black and later turn to glittering golden orange and sometimes to opalescent white. Some of the shubunkins and the calico fantails have transparent scales that look like thin skin. They display an assortment of colors such as red, yellow, orange, purple, pink, black, and blue.

Goldfish and koi will produce some young if they have submerged or floating plants to spawn on. The fish population will expand or contract in accordance with a number of factors, such as water quality and how much you feed them. If you give them a lot of food, they'll feel there's enough for more; they will produce more babies, thus creating the problem of over-population. But nature deals with this, too. The presence of too many fish inhibits spawning, and the fish eat some of the eggs and the fry. Moreover, as with other creatures, crowding makes the population more susceptible to diseases and parasites.

If you wish to produce plenty of goldfish to give away or to stock another pond, place a spawning mat in the pond in the spring when the temperature is between 50 and 60 degrees. Goldfish prefer to mate between sunrise and noon. The eggs are the diameter of a pinhead and are white with a hint of gray amber. When the fish have finished spawning for the day, move the mat to an unstocked pond. The fry will hatch in three to seven days. Warmer temperatures hasten hatching, and cooler temperatures delay it. Feed the fry crumbled flake fish food.

Golden Orfe

Golden orfe, *Leuciscus idus,* are pretty European fish, almost cylindrical, that swim near the surface fast and jump for insects. Unlike goldfish and koi, which swim along lazily, orfe are in constant motion, swimming all together in a school. Orfe lay their eggs on a bed of gravel or stones rather than in vegetation, but in a water garden they don't spawn as readily as goldfish. If you don't supply gravel, their numbers will not

Remarkably intelligent fish, koi have a certain sense of dignity and are known for their striking color variations. (Photo by Charles B. Thomas)

increase. Unfortunately, they are more sensitive to low levels of oxygen than goldfish and koi, so they do not survive as well in very warm water, for it contains less oxygen than cool water.

Koi

A koi, *Cyprinus carpio,* looks like a young comet or shubunkin, but the koi has a little whisker on either side of its mouth. Highly intelligent, koi can be trained to do tricks, even jump through hoops. When you buy young koi for a pond you are getting mixed varieties. But this special breed of colored carp, developed in Japan, is the focus of many books, societies, and competitions. Koi fanciers breed thirteen standard varieties and many subdivisions, based on a Japanese naming system dealing with color, color patterns, and scale formation.

Under usual conditions, koi will not jump after their first few days in a pond. They have a certain sense of dignity and would rather nibble new leaves down below than leap for insects. If you have koi, you must protect the submerged plants with a plastic mesh. At the U.S. National Arboretum in Washington, the water lilies survive among 2- and 3-foot koi because they are well fed and the tops of the pots are only 4 inches below the surface. Koi under 6 or 7 inches are usually compatible with normally planted water lilies. These fish avoid shallow surface areas where their bright colors expose them to predators.

Snails

Some people think slugs are snails that have left their shells — not so. And snails do not bring on slugs! The black Japanese snail, *Viviparus malleatus*, won't eat the plants and will not leave the pond. It gives birth to living young once or twice during the season. Other aquatic snails are egg layers and in a water garden tend to become overpopulated and eat the plants. (Fortunately, some have soft shells and the koi eat them.)

One black Japanese snail for every 1 or 2 square feet of water surface will help to keep the pond clear of food the fish have missed, as well as fish waste, undesirable algae, and dead leaves. They clean the submerged pots, travel up and down the stems of water lilies, grazing on the algae there, and take out extraneous material the pump and filter would otherwise have to handle. Some pond owners make pets of their snails, which are fascinating little creatures. They live year after year, balancing their numbers in an appropriate fashion with no special aid from the owner. They are most at risk from raccoons.

During the winter, snails, like fish and tadpoles, become dormant.

Tadpoles and Frogs

Tadpoles of the bullfrog, *Rana catesbeiana*, are shipped in spring and fall for water gardens. As tadpoles the first summer they'll help clear the pond of algae and uneaten fish food. The next year, around the time spring turns to summer, they will begin to turn into bullfrogs. As adults they'll provide evensong and gobble insects in commendable fashion. If they're not getting enough to eat, from time to time one may follow its natural instincts and go fishing for supper. The fish population will soon replace the missing members. Frogs live in the water but like to sun themselves on lily pads. In the frost belt, as

Oscar belongs to Mary Evans, of Washington, D.C. Unlike most bullfrogs, he is a homebody. (Photo by Mary Evans)

winter approaches they bury themselves in the mud and remain dormant all winter.

For some water garden owners, the frogs they bring in
or attract from the wild are the pond's best feature. But frogs
aren't as easily trained as goldfish and, ignoring human affection, may move to someone else's pond.

Turtles — Only for Love

Turtles are not recommended for water gardens. Only turtle
fanciers put them into planted ponds. They are interesting little
reptiles that come up to breathe air and need a place where
they can get into and out of the pond and also sunbathe.
Scavengers, they eat table scraps, submerged plants, and dead
fish — or live fish if they are hungry and other food isn't
readily available. They also are in the habit of snipping off the
stems of water lily blossoms and pads, though they don't eat
them. If you see a floating leaf that has been severed from the
plant as though by scissors or a knife, it is a sign that an aquatic
turtle has chosen your pond for its home. They may roam,
especially in rainy weather. In winter they bury themselves in
mud as the frogs do and remain dormant. If you must have a
turtle, be sure that your water lilies are well established before
you introduce it into your pond.

Hardiness Zone Map

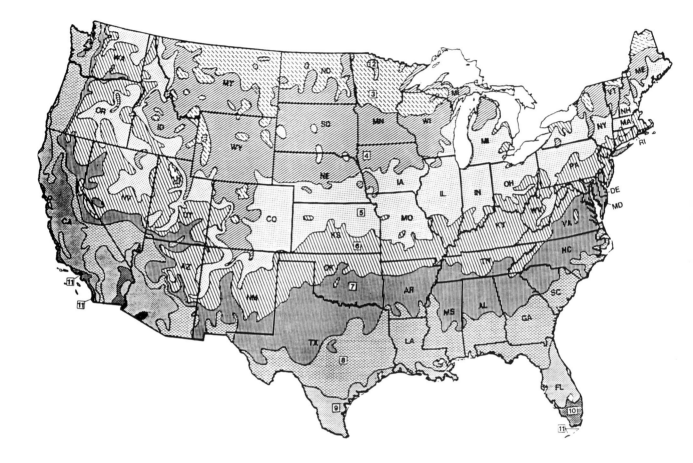

Range of Average Annual Minimum Temperatures for Each Zone

ZONE 1	BELOW		−50°F
ZONE 2	−50°	TO	−40°
ZONE 3	−40°	TO	−30°
ZONE 4	−30°	TO	−20°
ZONE 5	−20°	TO	−10°
ZONE 6	−10°	TO	0°
ZONE 7	0°	TO	10°
ZONE 8	10°	TO	20°
ZONE 9	20°	TO	30°
ZONE 10	30°	TO	40°
ZONE 11	ABOVE		40°

Appendix: Pronunciation of Botanical Names

Acorus calamus
Ak'or-us kal'am-us

Alisma plantago-aquatica
Al-iz'muh plan-tay'go ah-kwat'ik-uh

Aponogeton distachyus
Ah-poh-no-jee'tun dis-tak'ee-us

Azolla caroliniana
Ah-zoll'uh ka-ro-lin-ee-ay'nuh

Butomus umbellatus
Bew'toe-mus um-bell-lot'us

Cabomba caroliniana
Ka-bom'ba ka-ro-lin-ee-ay'nuh

Canna × hybrida
Can'nuh ex high'brid-uh

Ceratopteris pteridoides
ser-ah-top'ter-iss ter-id-doi'id-eez

Chasmanthium latifolium
Kas-man'thee-um lat-if-foh'lee-um

Colocasia
Kol-oh-kay'see-uh

   C. affinis var. *Jenningsii*
   C. aff-in'iss var. jen-ning-see'eye

   C. esculenta
   C. es-kew-lent'uh

   C. e. var. *fontanesii*
   C. e. var. font-ah-nay'zee-eye

Cotula coronopifolia
Ko'tew-luh core-oh-nop-ih-foh'lee-uh

Crinum americanum
Krye'num ah-mare-ee-kahn'um

Cyperus
Sye-peer'us

   C. alternifolius
   C. al-ter-nih-foh'lee-us

   C. haspan
   C. has'pan

   C. papyrus
   C. pap-eye'rus

Dulichium arundinaceum
due-lick'ee-um a-run-dih-nah'see-um

Eichhornia
Ike-hor'nee-uh

   E. crassipes
   E. krass'ih-peez

   E. paniculata
   E. pan-ik-kew-lay'tuh

Eleocharis
El-ee-oh-cair'iss

   E. montevidensis
   E. mon-tih-vid-den'siss

   E. tuberosa
   E. too'bay-roh'suh

Elodea canadensis var. *gigantea*
El-oh-dee'ah can-a-den'sis var. jie-gan'tee-uh

Equisetum hyemale
Ek-wih-see'tum hi-mah'lay

Glyceria aquatica
Gly-see'ree-uh ah-kwat'ik-uh

Houttuynia cordata var. *variegata*
Ho-tew-ee′nee-uh kor-day′tuh var. vah-ree-uh-gat′uh

Hydrocleys nymphoides
Hy-drok′lees nim-foy′deez

Hymenocallis
Hy-men-oh-kal′iss

> *H. caribaea*
> H. kah-rib′ee-uh

> *H. liriosme*
> H. lih-ree-ohs′mee

Iris
Eye′riss

> *I. ensata* (synonym *kaempferi*)
> I. en-sat′uh

> *I. pseudacorus*
> I. su-dak′core-uss

> *I. sibirica*
> I. sigh-beer′ee-kuh

> *I. versicolor*
> I. ver′sih-kol-or

> *I. virginica*
> I. ver-jin′ik-uh

Lemna minor
Lem′nuh my′ner

Ludwigia sedioides
Lud-wee′jee-uh sed-ee-oy′deez

Lysimachia nummularia
Lye-sih-may′kee-uh num-yew-lay′ree-uh

Marsilea mutica
Mar-sill′ee-uh mew′tik-uh

Mentha aquatica
Men′thuh ah-kwat′ik-uh

Mimulus luteus
Mim′yew-lus lew′tee-us

Myriophyllum aquaticum
Meer-ee-oh-fill′um ah-kwat′ik-um

Nelumbo nucifera
Nay-lum′boh new-sif′er-uh

Nymphaea
Nim′fee-uh

N. colorata
N. co-loh-rah′tuh

N. odorata var. *gigantea*
N. oh-do-rah′tuh var. jie-gan′tee-uh

N. tetragona
N. tet-rah-gawn′uh

Nymphoides
nim-foy′deez

> *N. cristata*
> N. criss-tah′tah

> *N. geminata*
> N. jem-me-nah′tuh

> *N. peltata*
> N. pel-tah′tuh

Orontium aquaticum
Oh-ron′tee-um ah-kwat′ik-um

Panicum virgatum
Pan′ik-um ver-gay′tum

Peltandra virginica
Pel-tand′ruh ver-jin′ik-uh

Pennisetum alopecuroides
Pen-is-see′tum aloe-pek-yew-roy′deez

Pistia stratiotes
Pis′tee-uh strat-ee-yo′teez

Pontederia cordata
Pon-tay-dare′ee-uh kor-dah′tuh

Sagittaria
saj-it-tay′ree-uh

> *S. lancifolia* form *ruminoides*
> S. lan-see-foh′lee-uh form rue-mi-noy′deez

> *S. latifolia*
> S. lat-if-foh′lee-uh

> *S. montevidensis*
> S. mon-tih-vid-den′siss

> *S. sagittifolia* 'Flore Pleno'
> S. sah-jit-ih-foh′lee-uh flo-reh plee-no

> *S. subulata*
> S. sub-yew-lay′tah

Salvinia auriculata
Sal-vin′ee-uh aw-rik-yew-lay′tah

Saururus cernuus
Saw-roo′rus sir-noo′us

Scirpus tabernaemontani 'Albescens'
Sir′puss tab-burr-nay-mon-tan′ee al-bess′enz

Thalia
Thay′lee-uh

   T. dealbata
   T. del-bah′tuh

   T. geniculata var. *ruminoides*
   T. jen-ik-kew-lay′tuh var. rue-mi-noy′deez

Typha
Tye′fuh

   T. angustifolia
   T. an-gus-tif-foh′lee-uh

   T. latifolia
   T. lah-ti-foh′lee-uh

   T. laxmannii
   T. lax-man′nee-eye

Vallisneria americana
val-lis-near′ree-ah ah-mare-ih-kahn′ah

Victoria cruziana
vik-toh′ree-uh krew-zee-ay′nuh

Index

Page numbers in bold type refer to illustrations or main entries.

Acorus calamus (sweet flag, calamus), **184**
    'Variegatus' (variegated sweet flag), 18, **36**, 183, **184**
Aeration, 51, 54
Aerator, 79
Air pump, 44
Algae, 3, 7, 9, 10, 12, 37, **38–47**, 51, 55, 72, 73, 158, 173, 209, 210, 211, 213, 217, 218
Algicides, 42–44, 214
Alisma plantago-aquatica (water plantain), **195**
Alkalinity, 35
AlkaMinus, 45
AlkaPlus, 45
American lotus (*Nelumbo lutea*), 163, **166–67**
Ammonia, 39, 54, 212
Anacharis (*Elodea canadensis* var. *gigantea*), **46**, 54, **73–74**, 209
Anacharis canadensis (now *Elodea canadensis* var. *gigantea*), 73
Aponogeton distachyus (Water hawthorn), **144–45**
Arrowhead (*Sagittaria*), 71, 73, 158, **203–4**
    giant (*S. montevidensis*), **204**

Bacteria, 7, 39, 41, 54, 55, 76
    bottled, canned, 55, 76
Baking soda, 45
Balance in pond, 5, 7, 21, 22, 38, 40, 42, 51, **66–67**, 89, 143, 209, 210, 211, 212, 217
Bamboo, dwarf, 183
Bareroot plants, 76, 168
Birds, 3, 25, 37, 59
Birdsey, Dr. Monroe, 130
Black princess taro (*Colocasia affinis* var. *Jenningsii*), **197**
Blanketweed, 39
Blue flag (*Iris versicolor*), **181**
Blue lotus of the Nile (*Nymphaea caerula*), 162
Bog lily (*Crinum americanum*), 10, 193, **198**
Boise State University, 17
Brass-buttons (*Cotula coronopifolia*), 185
Brazilian pickerel rush (*Eichhornia paniculata*), **148, 200–1**
Broad-spectrum remedy, 76
Brooklyn Botanic Garden, 15
Bryne, Don, 125
Bubblers, 6, 37, 44, 51, **60**, 61, 65
Bullfrog (*Rana catesbeiana*), 12, **218–19**
Bulrush, white (*Scirpus tabernaemontani* 'Albescens'), **190**
Butterflies, 3, 25, 37
Butomus umbellatus (flowering rush), **185**

Cabomba caroliniana (Washington grass), **73**, 209
Calamagrostis acutiflora 'Stricta' (feather reed grass), 192
Calamus (*Acorus calamus*), **184**
Calamus root, 184

Calico fantail, **214–15**
Canna
    × *hybrida*, **160**, 193, **195–96**
    Longwood, **148**, 194, **195–96**
    variegated (*C. americanallis* var. *variegata*), 19, 195
Cape blue water lily (*Nymphaea* 'Blue Capensis'), **125**
Carassius auratus (goldfish), 21, 25, 35, 44, 67, 71, 77, 80, 193, **208–9**, 212, **213**, **214–15**, 216, 219
    calico fantail, 214–15
    comet, 214–15, 216
    Japanese fantail, 15, **208**, 214–15
    Shubunkin, **208**, **214–15**, 216
Carbon dioxide, 12, 63
Cats, 25, 211
Cattail (*Typha*), 10, 21, **40**, **62**, **190**, **142–43**, **172–73**, 183, **190–92**
    graceful (*T. laxmannii*), **192**
    narrow-leaved (*T. angustifolia*), 160, **191**
    variegated (*T. latifolia* var. *variegata*), **192**
Ceratopteris pteridoides (floating fern), **145**
Chameleon plant (*Houttuynia* var. *variegata*), **201**
Changeable water lilies, 92, **93**, 96, 100, 165
Chasmanthium latifolium (northern oats), 192
Chinese water chestnut (*Eleocharis tuberosa*), **187**
Chloramine, 17, 47
Chlorine, 47, 67
Chlorine dioxide, 48
Colocasia (elephant's-ear), 75, 193, **196–97**
    affinis var. *Jenningsii* (black princess taro), **197**
    esculenta (taro), **21, 197**
        'Hilo Beauty', 197
        var. *fontanesii* (violet-stemmed taro), **197**
Comet (goldfish), **214–15**, 216
Containers, 18, 22, **68–69**, 70–71, 79, 154, 173, 174, 194, 199, 206
Coping, 24, 25, 31, **32–33**, 34, **35**
Cornell University, 86
Cotula coronopifolia (brass-buttons), **185**
Creeping Jennie (*Lysimachia nummularia*), 149
Crinum americanum (bog lily), 10, 193, **198**
Cultivar names, 85
Cyperus (cyperus), **198–200**
    alternifolius (umbrella palm), **142**, **172–73**, 194, **199**
    haspan (dwarf papyrus), **10–11**, 194, **199–200**
    papyrus (Egyptian paper reed), **199–200**
Cyprinus carpio (koi), 25, 44, 51, 57, 64, 67, 71, 77, 209, 210, 212, 215, **216–17**

Dade Community College, 130
Dechlorinating water, 37, 38, **47–48**, 79
Deer, 25

De-icer, 63, 77
Designing the pond, **22**
Diseases
    fish, 45, 76, 209, 212
    plant, 92
Dragonflies, 3, 25
Drainage, 16, 68
Dreer, Henry A., 104
Duck potato (*Sagittaria latifolia*), **204**
Dulichium arundinaceum (dwarf bamboo), 183, **185**
Dwarf bamboo (*Dulichium arundinaceum*), 183, **185**
Dwarf papyrus (*Cyperus haspan*), 10, 194, **199–200**
Dwarf sagittaria (*Sagittaria subulata*), 71, 73, **74**
Dye, black, 41, **42**

Earth-bottomed ponds, 6
East Indian lotus (*Nelumbo nucifera*), 163, **168**
Ecosystem of the pond, 5, 7, 8, 9
Egyptian lotus (*Nymphaea caerula*), 162
Egyptian paper reed (*Cyperus papyrus*), **199**
Egyptian white lotus (*Nymphaea lotus*), 162
Eichhornia
    crassipes (water hyacinth), 73, 144, **145–46**, 154,
      200
    paniculata (Brazilian pickerel rush), 148, **200–1**
Eleocharis (spike rush), **186–87**, 200
    montevidensis (spike rush), **187**, 200
    tuberosa (Chinese water chestnut), 187
Elephant's-ear (*Colocasia*), 75, 193, **196–97**
Elodea canadensis var. *gigantea* (anacharis), **73–74**, 209
Equisetum hyemale (horsetail), 21, 75, 183, **187–88**
Esmonde-White, Anstace and Larry, 26
European water clover (*Marsilea quadrifolia*), 149
Evans, Mary, 218
Everglades Aquatic Nurseries, 130

Fantail, Japanese, 15, **208–9**, 214–15
Feather reed grass (*Calamagrostis acutiflora* 'Stricta'), 192
Federal wetlands laws, 73, 145
Fencing, 18, 20
Fertilizing, aquatic plants, **69–70**, 72, 78, 80, 116, 132,
    139, 140, 155, 206, 210
Filters, 6, 37, 41, 42, 51, **52–55**, 57, 59, 60, 65, 73, 75,
    78, 79, 81, 214
    biological, 38, 41, 53–55, 81, 214
    mechanical, 52–53
Fish food, 39, 51, 210, 211, 218
    antibiotic, 77
Fish count. *See* Magic formula
Fish waste, 39, 51, 211, 212
Floating fern (*Ceratopteris pteridoides*), 145
Floating-heart, yellow (*Nymphoides peltata*), 21, 144, **152**,
    172–73
Floating-leaved plants, **142–55**
Flowering rush (*Butomus umbellatus*), 185
Flowers, cutting, **90**, 97, 100, 103, 107, 110, 112, 123,
    161
Fountains, 15, 22, 51, 58, **62**

Fountain grass, rose (*Pennisetum alopecuroides*), 193
Fountainheads, 58
Formal pond, 22
Foxes, 25
Fragrance, 85, 88, 118, 139, 161
Fragrant floating-leaved plants
    Aponogeton distachyus, **144–45**
    Hydrocleys nymphoides, **146–47**
Fragrant marginals
    Acorus calamus, **184**
    Butomus umbellatus, **185**
    Crinum americanum, **198**
    Eleocharis montevidensis, **187**, 200
Fragrant lotus (all), 157, 161
    Nelumbo 'Alba Grandiflora', **166**
Fragrant hardy water lilies (*Nymphaea*)
    'Arc en Ciel', **112**, 113
    'Attraction', **13**, 92, **113**
    'Charlene Strawn', 90, 92, **99**
    'Charles de Meurville', **104**
    'Comanche', **100**
    'Escarboucle', **113–14**, **152–53**
    'Firecrest', **101**
    'Gladstone', **106**
    'Hermine', 94, **95**
    'Hollandia', 92, **110**
    'Indiana', **100**
    'James Brydon', 92, **104**, 158
    'Joey Tomocik', **100**
    'Marliacea Albida', 95, **98–99**, 106
    'Marliacea Carnea', **97**
    'Masaniello', **102**
    'Mayla', **110**, **111**
    'Mrs. C. W. Thomas', **111**
    odorata var. *gigantea*, **107**
    'Paul Hariot', 93, **96**
    'Perry's Fire Opal', **102**
    'Peter Slocum', **111–12**
    'Pink Beauty' (formerly 'Fabiola'), 89, 92, **96–97**
    'Pink Sensation', **102**, 108, 158, 163
    'Queen of Whites', **106**
    'Radiant Red', **105**
    'Rose Arey Hybrid', **112**
    'Rosy Morn', **103**
    'Sirius', **103**
    'Splendida', **103**
    'Sultan', **104**
    'Sumptuosa', **103**
    'Sunrise', **108**, **110**
    'Texas Dawn', **108**, **109–10**
    'Virginalis', 92, **107**, 158
    'Virginia', 85, 90, 92, **107–8**
Fragrant tropical water lilies (*Nymphaea*)
    'Afterglow', **130**
    'Blue Beauty', 120, **132**, **133**, 158
    'Charles Thomas', 120, **122**, **123**
    'General Pershing', 120, **130**, 131
    'Golden West', **125**

'Jack Wood', **131**
'Marian Strawn', 120, **121**
'Maroon Beauty', **137**
'Mrs. C. W. Ward', **132**
'Mrs. George H. Pring', **128**
'Pink Perfection', **131**
'Red Flare', **91**, 120, **136**, 137, 158
Victoria cruziana, 78, **84**, **138–39**
Fragrant water lily (*Nymphaea odorata* var. *gigantea*), 107
Frogs, 7, 12, **13**, 22, 25, 76, 210, 211, **218–19**
Fungus on fish, 76

Game fish, 44
Glyceria aquatica 'Vanelson', 192
Golden buttons (*Cotula coronopifolia*), 185
Golden-club (*Orontium aquaticum*), **202**
Golden orfe (*Leuciscus idus*), 44, 67, 77, 209, **215–16**
Goldfish (*Carassius auratus*), 21, 25, 35, 44, 67, 71, 77, 80, 193, **208–9**, 212, **213**, **214–15**, 216, 219
Graceful cattail (*Typha laxmannii*), **192**
Gravel, rinsed, 70, 72
Green water, 37, **40**, 42, 67
Ground-fault circuit interrupter, 57, 61, 63

Hawks, 25
Horsetail (*Equisetum hyemale*), 21, 75, 183, **187–88**
Houttuynia var. *variegata* (chameleon plant), **201**
Hydrocleys nymphoides (water poppy), 144, **146–47**
Hymenocallis
  caribaea var. *variegata* (variegated spider lily), **188**
  liriosme (spider lily), 183, **188–89**

Ice, **63**, 80, 116
Installing the water garden, **25–35**
International Water Lily Hall of Fame, 86
Insulation, 80
Iris, 4, 10, 21, 22, **70**, 75, **174–82**, 183
  Japanese (*Iris ensata*), 176, **181–82**
  Louisiana, 176, **177–79**
    'Black Gamecock', **178**
    'Bryce Leigh', **179**
    'Clyde Redmond, **178–79**
    'Dixie Deb', **178**
    'Eolian', **179**
    'Her Highness', **178**
    'Marie Caillet', **178**
  Red (*I. fulva*), **177**
  Siberian (*Iris sibirica*), 176, **179–81**
Iris, 4, 10, 21, 70, 75; **174–83**
  I. ensata (syn. *kaempferi*) (Japanese iris), 176, **181–82**
  I. foliosa, 177
  I. fulva (red iris), **177**
  I. giganticaerulea, 177
  I. pseudacorus (yellow flag), **175**, **176–77**, 195
    'Flora Plena', 176
    variegated, **176**, 183
  I. sibirica (Siberian iris), 176, **179–81**

I. versicolor (blue flag), **181**
I. virginica (swamp flag), 181

Japanese fantail, 15, **208–9**, 214–15
Japanese garden, **14–15**, 22
Japanese iris, 176, **181–82**
Japanese koi, 210
Japanese snail (*Viviparus malleatus*), 12, **217**

Kenilworth Aquatic Gardens, 140–41, 169
Kettle garden, 16, 150, 164, 183, 194
Koi (*Cyprinus carpio*), 44, 51, 57, **64**, 67, 71, 77, 209, 210, 212, 215, **216–17**

Landon, Kenneth, 110
Ledbetter, Gordon, 56
Leuciscus idus (golden orfe), 44, 67, 77, 209, **215–16**
Lighting, **61–63**
Lilypons Water Gardens, 68, 127, 136, 169
Lily pruning tool, 115
Lime, 35
Lizard's-tail (*Saururus cernuus*), 194, **204–5**
Longwood canna (*Canna* × *hybrida*), **148**, 194, **195–96**
Longwood Gardens, 42, 85, 138, 148, 160, 195
Lotus (*Nelumbo*), 16, 23, 70, 78, 85, **148**, **157–71**, 193
  cultivars
    'Alba Grandiflora', **166**
    'Charles B. Thomas', **164**
    'Chawan Basu', **164**
    'Momo Botan', 164, **165**
    'Momo Botan Minima', **163–64**
    'Mrs. Perry D. Slocum, **156**, 158, 163, 165, **167**, 168
    'Red Lotus', **168**
    'Roseum Plenum', 163, **165**
    'Shirokunshi', 163
    Tulip Lotus, 158, **163**, 164
Lotusland (California), 124
Louisiana iris, 176, **177–79**
Ludwigia sedioides (ludwigia), **148–49**
Lysimachia nummularia (creeping Jennie), 149
  'Aurea', 149

Magic formula, 41, 65, **66–67**, 75, 210
Maiden grass (*Miscanthus sinensis* 'Gracillimus'), 193
Marginal plants, **173–209**
Marliac, Latour, 86, 96, 97, 112, 113
Marsilea
  mutica (four-leaf water clover), **149**, 158
  quadrifolia (European water clover), 149
Measurements, pond, **48–49**
Mentha
  aquatica (water mint), **201–2**
  × *piperita* (peppermint), 201
  × *piperita* var. *citrata*, 201

Milfoil, water (*Myriophyllum*), **19**, 54, **74**
Mimulus luteus (monkey flower), **189**
Minnows, 25
Mint, water (*Mentha aquatica*), **201–2**
Miscanthus sinensis 'Gracillimus' (maiden grass), 193
Missouri Botanic Garden, 86, 128
Monkey flower (*Mimulus luteus*), **189**
Montreal Botanic Garden, 175
Moore, George T., 128
Mortar, 35
Mosquitoes, 12, 19, 210
Moving pond plants, 71
Myriophyllum (water milfoil), **19**, 54, **74**
Myriophyllum aquaticum (parrot's feather), 18, **19**, 74, **142–43**, **150**, 173

Narrow-leaved cattail (*Typha angustifolia*), 160, **191**
National Aquatic Gardens, 41
National Park Service, 140
Naturalized pond, 22
Nelson, Rolf, 136
Nelumbo (lotus) (*see also* Lotus: cultivars), 16, 23, 70, 78, **85**, **148**, **157–71**, 193
    lutea (American lotus), 163, **166–67**
    nucifera (sacred lotus), 157, 163, **168**
Nitrates, 39, 41, 54
Nitrites, 39, 212
Nitrogen, 37, 211
    cycle, 39
Northern oats (*Chasmanthium latifolium*), 192
Nymphaea (water lilies) (*see also* Water lily cultivars), **85–141**
    caerula (Egyptian lotus), 162
    capensis, **131**
    colorata, **121**
    lotus (Egyptian white lotus), 162
    odorata var. *gigantea* (fragrant water lily), **107**
    tetragona, **94**
        'Helvola', 95
Nymphaeaceae, 138
Nymphoides, **150–52**
    crenata (yellow snowflake), 144, **151**
        N. c. var. (orange snowflake), **152**
    cristata (white snowflake), 8, 144, **151–52**
    peltata (yellow floating-heart), 144, **152**, 173

Orange snowflake (*Nymphoides crenata* var.), **152**
Orchid iris (*Iris ensata*), 181
Orfe, golden (*Leuciscus idus*), 44, 67, 77, 209, **215–16**
Ornamental grasses, 10, **193–94**
Orontium aquaticum (golden-club), **202**
Oxygen, 7, 9, 12, 19, **44**, 51, 54, 63, 79, 211, 216

Pagels, Walter, 205
Panicum virgatum (switch-grass), 193

Papyrus, **198–99**
    dwarf (*Cyperus haspan*), **10–11**, 194, **199–200**
Parrot's feather (*Myriophyllum aquaticum*), 18, **19**, 74, **142–43**, **150**, **172–73**
Peltandra virginica (water arum), 194, **202–3**
Pennisetum alopecuroides (rose fountain grass), 193
pH, 12, 35, **45–47**, 68–69, 70, 180, 182, 212
Pickerel rush (*Pontederia cordata*), 21, **36–37**, **62**, **142–43**, 194, **203**
Pistia stratiotes (water lettuce), 144, **152–54**
Plants (*see also* Propagation)
    placing, **70–71**
    planting, 65, **67–71**
Platforms, 70, 194
"Polishing" water, 54
Pond capacity, in gallons, **48–49**
Pond liners, 24, **25–35**, 60
Pond maintenance, 65, **78–81**
Pond nuts (*Nelumbo lutea*), 163, **166**
Pond shelf, **25–35**, 70, 194, 206
Pontederia cordata (pickerel rush), 21, **36–37**, **62**, **142–43**, 194, **203**
Possums, 25
Predators, 17, 25
Pring, George H., 86, 128, 129, 134, 136, **138**
Propagation, 94, 116–17, 120, 139, 145, 150, 169, 170–71, 181, 182–83, 185, 188, 190, 198–99, 203, 207, 210
Pump power (table), 58
Pumps, 6, 19, 42, 44, 51, **55–59**, 60, 61, 62, 79, 81
    adapter for, 57
    air, 44
    recirculating, 6, 42, 44, 51
Pygmy water lilies, 94, 115

Raccoons, 17, 18, 25, 211, 217
Rain, effect of, 45
Rana catesbeiana (bullfrog), **218–19**
Randig, Evelyn, 125
Randig, Martin E., 86, 125
Red iris (*Iris fulva*), **177**
Red spots on fish, 76
Red-stemmed sagittaria (*Sagittaria lancifolia* forma *ruminoides*), **189–90**
Red-stemmed thalia (*Thalia geniculata* var. *ruminoides*), **205–6**
Root-bound plants, 116
Rose fountain grass (*Pennisetum alopecuroides*), 193

Sacred lotus (*Nelumbo nucifera*), 157, 163, **168**
Sagittaria, 71, 73, **74**, 158, 183, **189–90**, **203–4**
    japonica (*S. sagittifolia* 'Flore Pleno'), 204
    lancifolia forma *ruminoides* (red-stemmed sagittaria), **189–90**
    latifolia (arrowhead), **159**, 204
    montevidensis (giant arrowhead), 204
    sagittifolia 'Flore Pleno' (double old-world arrowhead), 204
    subulata (dwarf sagittaria), 71, 73, **74**

Saururus cernuus (lizard's-tail), 194, **204–5**
Scavengers. *See* Frogs; Snails; Turtles
Scirpus tabernaemontani 'Albescens' (white bulrush), 190
Shubunkins (goldfish), **208**, **214–15**, 216
Siberian iris (*Iris sibirica*), 176, **179–81**
Silt, 79
Siting the pond, **14–35**
Slocum, Perry, 86, 98, 102, 111, 163, 164
Snails, 3, 12, 17, 19, 66, 67, 76, 79, 209, 210, **217**
    Japanese (*Viviparus malleatus*), 12, 66, **217**
Snakes, 211
Snowflake (*Nymphoides*), **150–52**
    orange (*N. c.*var.), **152**
    white (*N. cristata*), **8**, **144**, 151, **152**
    yellow (*N. crenata*), 144, **151**
Snowflake, water (*Nymphoides cristata*), **144**, **151–52**
Sod, 32
Soil for aquatic plants, 68–70, 72, 74, 115, 139, 145, 180, 182, 198
Spawning, fish, **8**, 146, 210, 215
Spider lily (*Hymenocallis liriosme*), 183, **188–89**
    variegated (*H. caribaea* var. *variegata*), **188**
Spike rush (*Eleocharis montevidensis*), **186–87**, 200
Spray(s) (fountain), 6, 61
Sprinklers, effect of, 17
Star lilies, 132
Statuary, 6, 22, 44, 58, 61, 65
Statues, **51**, 58, **62**, 193
Stocking the water garden, 65, **76–78**
Strawn, Dr. Kirk, 86, 99, 100, 110, 121
Submerged plants, **7, 8, 18, 38, 39, 40, 41, 42, 46**, 54, **64, 66–67**, 68, **71–76**, 79, 145, 150, 210, 211, 212, 214, 215, 217, 219
Surface size of pond, **48–49**
Swamp flag (*Iris virginica*), 181
Sweet flag (*Acorus calamus*), **184**
    variegated (*A. c.* 'Variegatus'), 18, 36, 183, **184**
Switch-grass (*Panicum virgatum*), 193

Tadpoles, 7, 12, 77, 210, 217, **218–19**
Taro (*Colocasia esculenta*) 21, 75, **196–97**
    black princess (*C. affinis* var. *Jenningsii*), **197**
    violet-stemmed (*C. esculenta* var. *fontanesii*), **197**
Temple-sur-Lot (France), 86
Thalia (Thalia), 193, **205–6**
    dealbata, 160, 194, **205**
    geniculata var. *ruminoides* (red-stemmed thalia), **205–6**
Thermostats, 63
Thomas, Charles B., 108, 111
Thomas, George L., Jr., 127
Thomas, Virginia, 108
Transformer, for lighting, 61
Tubs, 15, 16, 19, 22, 67, 78, 94, 96, 121, 124, 127, 128, 130, 132, 140, 158, 164, 166, 183, 186, 194
Tubers, 121, 139, 141, 158, 161, 168–69, 204

Tulip lotus, 158, 162, **163**
Turtles, 211, **219**
Typha (cattail), 10, 21, **40, 62**, **142–43**, **172–73**, 183, **190–92**
    angustifolia (narrow-leaved cattail), 160, **191**
    latifolia (cattail), **192**
        var. *variegata*, (variegated cattail), **192**
    T. laxmannii (graceful cattail), **192**

Umbrella palm (*Cyperus alternifolius*), 142–43, **173**, 193, 194, **199**
Underlayment for pond liner, 26, 32
U.S. National Arboretum, 41, 217

Vallisneria americana (wild celery), 71, **75**
Variegated canna (*Canna americanallis* var. *variegata*), 19, **195**
Variegated cattail (*Typha latifolia* var. *variegata*), **192**
Variegated spider lily (*Hymenocallis caribaea* var. *variegata*), **188**
Variegated sweet flag (*Acorus calamus* 'Variegatus'), 18, **36**, 183, **184**
Variegated yellow flag (*Iris pseudacorus*), 176, 183
Verticals (marginals), 173, **209**
Victoria
    amazonica, 138
    cruziana, 78, **84**, **138–39**
    'Longwood', 138
Violet-stemmed taro (*Colocasia esculenta* var. *fontanesii*), **197**
Viviparous water lilies, 119, 120, 122, 123, 124, 125, 127
Volume of pond, **48–49**

Wanquakin (*Nelumbo lutea*), 166
Washington grass (*Cabomba caroliniana*), 73, 209
Water arum (*Peltandra virginica*), 194, **202–3**
Water canna, **160**
Water chinquapin (*Nelumbo lutea*), 166
Water clover
    European (*Marsilea quadrifolia*), 149
    four-leaf (*Marsilea mutica*), 21, **149**, 158
Watercourse, 24, 51, 58, 60
Waterfall, 6, 23, 24, **36, 37, 44**, 51, 54, **56**, 58, 59–61, 65, 150
Water fringe (*Nymphoides peltata*), 152
Water hawthorn (*Aponogeton distachyus*), **144**
Water hyacinth (*Eichhornia crassipes*), 73, 144, **145–46**, 154, 200
Water lettuce (*Pistia stratiotes*), 73, 144, **152–54**
Water lily (*Nymphaea*) cultivars, hardy, **90–117**
    'Arc en Ciel', **112**, 113
    'Attraction', **13**, 92, **113**
    'Charlene Strawn', 90, 92, **99**
    'Charles de Meurville', **104**
    'Chromatella', **91**, 92, **96**
    'Comanche', 92, **100**
    'Ellisiana', **97**
    'Escarboucle', **113–14**, **152–53**
    'Firecrest', **101**

Water lily (*Nymphaea*) cultivars, hardy (*cont.*)
  'Gladstone', **106**
  'Gloire de Temple-sur-Lot', 86, 87, **112**
  'Gonnere', **98**
  'Hermine', **94, 95**
  'Hollandia', 92, **110**
  'Indiana', **100**
  'James Brydon', 92, **104**, 158
  'Joey Tomocik', **100**
  'Marliacea Albida', 95, **98–99**, 106
  'Marliacea Carnea', **97**
  'Masaniello', **102**
  'Mayla', **110, 111**
  'Mrs. C. W. Thomas', **111**
  'Paul Hariot', **93, 96**
  'Perry's Dwarf Red', **98**
  'Perry's Fire Opal', **102**
  'Peter Slocum', **111–12**
  'Pink Beauty' (formerly 'Fabiola'), 89, 92, **96–97**
  'Pink Sensation', **102**, 108, 158, 163
  'Queen of Whites', **106**
  'Radiant Red', **105**
  'Rose Arey Hybrid', **112**
  'Rosy Morn', **103**
  'Sioux', **93, 100**
  'Sirius', **103**
  'Splendida', **103**
  'Sultan', **104**
  'Sumptuosa', **103**
  'Sunrise', **108, 109–10**
  'Texas Dawn', **108, 109**
  'Virginalis', 92, **107**, 158
  'Virginia', 85, 90, 92, **107–8**
  'William Falconer', **106**
Water lily (*Nymphaea*) cultivars, tropical day-blooming, **121–33**
  'Albert Greenberg', **130**
  'Afterglow', **130**
  'Aviator Pring', **128–29**
  'Blue Beauty', 120, **132, 133**, 158
  'Blue Capensis', **125**
  'Blue Star', **133**
  'Blue Triumph', 120, **126**
  'Charles Thomas', 120, **122, 123**
  'Dauben', 18, 89, 119, 120, **121–23**, 125, 127
  'Director George T. Moore', **127**, 128, 132
  'General Pershing', 120, **130, 131**
  'Golden West', **125**
  'Hilary', **123**
  'Jack Wood', **131**
  'Leopardess', **126**
  'Madame Ganna Walska', 120, **124**
  'Margaret Mary', **127**
  'Marian Strawn', 120, **121**
  'Mrs. C. W. Ward', **132**
  'Mrs. George H. Pring', **128**
  'Mrs. Martin E. Randig', 120, **124**
  'Panama Pacific', **124**
  'Pink Capensis', **131**
  'Pink Pearl', 120, **131**
  'Pink Perfection', **131**
  Pink Star (sic), 132
  'Robert Strawn', **123**
  'Shirley Bryne', **125**
  'White Delight', 120, **128**
  'Wood's Blue Goddess', **132–33**
  'Yellow Dazzler', **128**
Water lily (*Nymphaea*) cultivars, tropical night-blooming, **133–47**
  'Emily Grant Hutchings', 120, **134–35**, 136
  'Green Smoke', 119
  'H. C. Haarstick', **137**
  'Maroon Beauty', **137**
  'Missouri', **133**
  'Mrs. George Hitchcock', **136**
  'Red Flare', **91**, 120, **136**, 137, 158
  'Texas Shell Pink', 120, **136**
  'Wood's White Knight', 89, 119, 120, **134, 137**
Water lily leaves, juvenile, 92
Water milfoil (*Myriophyllum*), **19**, 54, **74**
Water mint (*Mentha aquatica*), **201–2**
Water-nymph, 85
Water pickerel rush, 194
Water plantain (*Alisma plantago-aquatica*), **195**
Water poppy (*Hydrocleys nymphoides*), 144, **146–47**
Water snowflake (*Nymphoides cristata*), 152
Wetlands regulations, 6
White bulrush (*Scirpus tabernaemontani* 'Albescens'), **190**
White snowflake (*Nymphoides cristata*), 8, 144, **151–52**
Wild celery (*Vallisneria americana*), 71, **75**
Wildlife, 15, 18, **24–25**, 42
Winch, Charlie, 128
Winter care of plants, 20, 55, 57, 65, 72, 78, **80–81**, 92, 94, 104, **116, 139–41**, 144, 147, 149, **154–55**, 161, 165, **168–69**, 178, **182–83**, 185, 190, 199, **207, 214**, 217, 219
Wood, Jack, 86, 123, 133

Yanquapin (*Nelumbo lutea*), **166**
Yellow flag (*Iris pseudacorus*), 175, **176–77**
  variegated, **176**, 183
Yellow floating-heart (*Nymphoides peltata*), 144, **152**, 173
Yellow lotus (*Nelumbo lutea*), **166**
Yellow snowflake (*Nymphoides crenata*), 144, **151–52**